Mexican Mornings

Mexican Mornings
Essays South of the Border

MICHAEL HOGAN

Introduction by Danny Root
Former U.S. Consul General, Guadalajara, Mexico

INTERCAMBIO PRESS

TRAFFORD

Cover photo: Ex-convento de Churubusco, courtesy of Lucinda Mayo

Published by INTERCAMBIO PRESS, San Diego, California, U.S.A.
In cooperation with Trafford Publishing, Victoria, B.C., Canada
Please direct orders and inquiries to Trafford Publishing
Suite 6E, 2333 Government St., Victoria, B.C. V8T 4P4 CANADA
Phone 250-383-6864 or toll-free 1-888-232-4444 (Canada & US)
Fax 250-383-6804   E-mail sales@trafford.com
Trafford Catalogue #01-0331
www.trafford.com   www.trafford.com/robots/01-0331.html

National Library of Canada Cataloguing in Publication Data
Hogan, Michael, 1943-
     Mexican mornings: essays south of the border
     ISBN 1-55212-929-2
     1. Mexico. I. Title.
F1227.H64 2001   972   C2001-902630-7

10   9   8   7   6   5   4   3

ACKNOWLEDGMENTS

Some of these essays first appeared in the following magazines: *Albany Review, Guadalajara Colony Reporter, Harvard Review. History Ireland, International Educator, The Nation, Newslinks, Ojo del Lago, Sin Fronteras, U.S. Catholic,* and *University of New Mexico Review.* Permission from the publishers to reprint is hereby gratefully acknowledged.

"The Bus From Hell or Going To See Fidel" was first published in the *Blue Mesa Review*, (formerly the *New Mexico Review*), Fall, 1993.

"The Great Kiskadee," "The Poet, "The Blind Men of Indostan," For Loving Fathers," and "Fort Adams" were originally published in *Sin Fronteras*.

"Green, I Love Thee, Green" first appeared in *Ojo del Lago* magazine in March, 1998.

"The Soldiers of St. Patrick" was originally published under the title "The Irish Soldiers of Mexico" in *History Ireland*, Vol. II, No. 6, 1998.

"On Canyons and Cancer Cells" was first published in the *Albany Review*, Spring, 1990.

"Permission To Speak" first appeared in the anthology *To Honor A Teacher*, ed. by Jeff Spoden. A & M Publications, 2000.

"Savage Capitalism" was originally published under the title "Liberation and Development: A Latin American Perspective" in the Sept. 12-16, 1999 issue of *The Guadalajara Colony Reporter*. A substantially revised version of this article also appeared in the June/July, 2000 issue of *Voices of Mexico*.

"Secret Gardens" was originally published under the title of "Going Back To Bisbee" in the *Harvard Review*, Winter, 1994.

"Judas Burning" was published in *Walking Rain Review*, Spring 2001. An earlier version received a *New Letters* Creative Non-Fiction Citation for the year 2000.

"Ask Me" copyright 1977, 1998 by the Estate of William Stafford. Reprinted from *The Way It Is: New and Selected Poems* with the permission of Graywolf Press, Saint Paul, Minnesota.

Ad Majorem Dei Gloriam

INTRODUCTION

There is a part of Mexico, the west-central area encompassing the state of Jalisco and its capital, Guadalajara, which is the cradle of many significant cultural traditions that most of us associate with that great country: mariachi music, tequila and *charreada* (rodeos) to name a few. Perhaps that is why the state's current government chose the slogan "Jalisco IS Mexico" to represent it before the world. And Jalisco is Michael Hogan's intellectual inspiration for this bird's eye view of Mexico and elsewhere.

Hogan writes with deep affection for his adopted country, mixed with an insider's keen interest about things Mexican. He adroitly highlights the best, and sometimes the worst, of life in this setting. The inexhaustible patience and forgiveness of the Mexican character is portrayed in many of his narratives, in which life is lived largely in the slow lane but with a degree of dignity and grace that might help explain why so many North Americans choose to call Mexico home.

This collection of essays is the first published non-fiction work by the author since his widely-acclaimed *Irish Soldiers of Mexico*, which was the basis for two documentaries and Orion's 1999 feature film, "One Man's Hero," starring Tom Berenger. A synopsis of that important, nearly forgotten piece of history is contained in this volume as "The Soldiers of St. Patrick."

The range of these essays takes us from Hogan's Catholic boyhood in Newport, Rhode Island to mid-life academia in Central Mexico, a world that is vastly different—or is it? The strength of a grandmother's love and a father's role in vanquishing monsters from a daughter's imagination could, and do, take place anywhere. But the insightful connection between the ancient Greek's philosophy of the man/woman relationship and Mexican "machismo," the reflection against history's mirror of the 1995 Chiapas "revolution," and the street-level view of the effect on Mexican society of NAFTA and Mexico's economic dependence on foreign investment, could only come from the Mexican heartland—and from a writer who is a serious observer of his environment and a perennial student of life.

Come ride with us on the Bus From Hell to see Cuban dictator Fidel Castro; and laugh at the drunken Santa Claus whose sleigh is damaged at the high school Christmas party. Then feel the beat of the music as the Tigres del Norte give an all-night concert in Guadalajara's immense Rio Nilo stadium; squint through the eyepiece of a welder's helmet during a solar eclipse; and squirm with uneasiness during a depression-producing six-day, six-night rainstorm.

Perhaps the strongest messages of this collection are those extolling the thoughts of Mexican diplomat and poet Octavio Paz, in helping understand ourselves; and those of environmentalist and writer Ed Abbey who tried to show all of us, of all nationalities, that if we want to save this world FOR ourselves, we first have to save it FROM ourselves.

So follow Hogan as he examines his subjects—from the lowest crawling insects that influence life in Jalisco as it is today, to the two-legged creatures of power that would change it forever. I promise you won't regret it.

Danny Root
Former U.S. Consul General
Guadalajara, Mexico

CONTENTS

THE CRAWLING THINGS OF PARADISE

In December in Jalisco the fields lie fallow in the sun. The dust motes fade as the sound of the tractor moves along the highway to the next *granja*. Although the desiccated corn stalks have been plowed under, other things are alive and grateful for the change. A snail moves purposely up the stalk of a fig tree by the wall. Bees cluster around the water trough: small, busy yellowjackets; the larger honeybees with their rounded black and gold bellies and furry ectoderms. Sometimes in great swarms the killer bees from the south come in clusters, black as oil smoke, and hover above the banana tree for an hour or more and then disappear. Their hum is that of an electrical transformer and they move like electrons too numerous to count or even see individually: deadly, predetermined, primal.

Around the *jefe's* hut in the *ejido* are gnats, smaller than mustard seeds, black, enamored of the eyes and ears. They buzz with a high-pitched whine as they enter the ear. Suicidally persistent, they could drive a saint crazy. Sometimes they, too, come in droves like the killer bees, insistent with some primordial purpose: at times, no larger than mere annoyance, on other occasions nothing less than the calculated insanity of their victims.

Beside each pool where the water drains from the cattle trough or the buckets in the hut, there are mosquitoes which one minute are busily drinking and the next searching for the blood of whoever (or whatever) is closest. Sailing among them like destroyers in the midst of fishing boats are the stately wasps. Their brown and gold bodies make them almost attractive in the midst of their frenetic neighbors. They derive sustenance from the cattle droppings and seem oblivious to people and animals.

Delicate and lighter than dandelion puffs, the phosphorescent dragonflies swoop through bees, gnats, mosquitos, wasps and assorted *bichos*. Angelic and rainbow-hued in the sun, they are neither negligible nor demure. They make love on the wing: joining bodies firmly, doing an aerial arabesque, and then swooping off together like perfectly matched figure skaters, or a pair of Blue Angels over the Nevada desert.

On the furrowed ground below them are black beetles, heavily armored, like tanks plodding over some eternal Bulge that has lasted through all the wars and rumors of war. Occasionally they stop and, with scissor claws and great sharp jaws, devour a mite, a flea or a mealy bug. Speaking of fleas… wherever there are animals here, there are fleas. They cling to the animals' hair, their soft underbellies. They jump with ease from animal to animal, animal to human. You find yourself scratching for them after even the most innocent and perfunctory walk through the *ejido*.

This time of year there are earwigs, too, which seem to be ubiquitous. There are earwigs in your bath towel in the morning when you get out of the shower. Earwigs drop on your head when you open the door to go to work. They have been hiding in the dark space between the door and the frame. They act as if you have disturbed them and not vice versa. There are earwigs in your book by the bedside at night. Occasionally, there are earwigs under your pillow.

Indigenous people here believe that earwigs are so named because they enter the ears—especially those of sleeping children—where they find the warm, moist tunnel attractive and comfortable. There they set up house, lay eggs, have babies, and—ultimately—drive the host child mad.

Over against the walls are piles of cuttings, branches, and compost that the workers have set aside. Hovering above them are horseflies, bluebottles, blackflies, gnats and hornets. Within the warm dampness of these innocuous heaps of decaying material are veritable tenements of insects. There are larvae, maggots, loopers and grubs. There are earth worms, dung beetles, aphids and red worms. There are velvety green worms and above them the Tricgogramma wasps which feed on the eggs the adult worms lay. There are the larvae of moths here, and also in the fruit trees nearby.

In the fruit trees, the female coddling moths release a pheromone (a scented hormone) which attracts the males. Creating similar formulae in the laboratory, scientists have been able to create new types of perfumes. More importantly for the farmers here, the scientists have also been able to duplicate the exact formula of the moth's pheromone. Using these the farmers have made pheromone traps which lure the male to his death, thus controlling the moth population. Besides these traps to protect the fruit trees, there are also large blue, box-like traps seen around the *ejido* (and throughout Mexico) used to capture and thus monitor the migration from the south of killer bees which daily grows larger.

There are anthills here and there which often remain undisturbed by the workers especially during the dry season. They live in great mounds and, it seems, kill many of the other predators on the farm. They frighten away some of the common parasites of the young, delicate plants. The ants themselves, however, in the rainy season become fearsome predators and then must be controlled.

There are praying mantises which eat the bees, and also eat each other. There are ladybugs which eat the aphids.

In the early evening there are nightflying moths which, when the moon is full, stop mating and laying eggs. Distracted and bewildered by the bright light of the moon, they dance in great numbers over the cornfield. A week or so later, however, they start mating at an increased rate and, by the time of the new moon, their larvae (corn earworms) are quite numerous.

The farmers here will plant their next maize crop early to avoid the later emerging moths. They will choose a variety of corn with tight husks to keep out the worms. They will not use chemicals to destroy them or risk poisoning the corn which is the staple of the Mexican diet.

There are mealy bugs, too, with white fuzzy bodies. There are red mites, yellow mites and green mites which at first look like specks of dust, but when seen closer can be observed moving. On even closer examination one sees that they have eight legs (they are tiny spider relatives) with a clear agenda.

Speaking of spiders... they are here, too. There is the ubiquitous daddy longlegs who spends much of his day catching flies and gnats. There is the brown recluse, deadly and silent. He is no friend to the inquisitive maid or the careless housewife. There is also the equally deadly black widow with her red-spotted warning.

There are weevils and slugs and scale insects. There are green fruitflies and black fruitflies which flourish indoors and out—all year long. There are whiteflies: winged adults and stationary pupae and nymphs which suck plant juices and exude a sticky substance which is, in fact, tiny eggs and freshly-hatched mobile young.

But the farmer does not spray for these either. He simply waits until the wasps lay their eggs in the whitefly nymphs and pupae. The wasp larvae hatch there and kill their hosts.

There are grasshoppers, too. There are cicadas which chant throughout the night rhythmically as one's breathing. There are crickets which are household pesticides if you do not mind their friendly chirping. Leave them alone, as well as the daddy longlegs and the occasional wasp, and you will obviate the need for the noxious (to insect and human alike) oil-based bug sprays sold in this area.

Still, no matter how tolerant one is, there are still more ants crawling across the mahogany table at dinner time than seems appropriate. The earwigs jumping out of the bath towel can certainly be disconcerting. And, even if one is as accepting and patient as Job, undisturbed by the chirping of the crickets or the ratcheting of the cicadas, there are nights when the high-pitched whine of a pair of mosquitos in the bedroom can make sleep impossible.

A friendly conversation in the backyard or garden can be a trial of bloodletting and self-flagellation as one slaps oneself senseless trying to keep the gnats out of the eyes, ears and nostrils. A casual walk though the *ejido* means a twenty minute shower examination with tweezers disengaging the vice grips of ticks, or shampooing out the fleas.

A horseback ride can be perilous, as your mount—enraged beyond control of the bit or your knees—bucks in a frenzy to rid himself of a throng of stinging horseflies. Three times as big as a housefly, the horsefly is green and black. Like anarchistic biker gangs they attack in virulent packs and their bite is no laughing matter. *¿Sabe montar?* in Jalisco means, "Do you know how to ride?" When they ask (and polite Mexicans always do), do not give a casual answer. It does not mean can you handle a horse walking calmly down a bridle path. It means can you handle a snorting stallion, eight hundred pounds rearing in the air, then striking off at a gallop down an arroyo before you can even think of the Spanish word for "whoa."

Mark Twain once wrote that the least of all the flies, the common housefly, was sufficient proof that a loving God could not have created the universe. Assuming there was a Creator, he wrote, it would have to have been a perverse, malicious entity to even conceive of such a maddening, useless insect. Imagine this Creator saying to himself: "Let me think of something ugly, bacteria-laden, annoying, repulsive and maddening, which will drive man from his contemplative serenity. I've got it. The housefly!"

Well, Twain, for all his humor and *joie de vivre*, was homocentric and narrow. He assumed that everything created had to do with man. He felt that the worth of anything in the universe was to be directly measured by its apparent utility or non-utility to humankind. Since no immediate human value could be readily ascribed to the housefly, he altered his theology to accommodate it. A bit simplistic. But not less different in substance from the dichotomy of the spotted owl and the lumber companies in Washington State, or the destruction of the "un-developed" rain forests in Brazil to create "productive" farmland.

That insects have value as part of a complex ecological system is beyond dispute and has been argued by biologists, naturalists and ecologists far more eloquently than I could even attempt. Still, the question remains to be dealt with on an aesthetic level. Such a wealth of insects is more than just mildly annoying. How is it that so many of us in this part of the world continue to not merely survive, but to live with genuine pleasure and enthusiasm?

A simple answer is... the birds. Where there are lots of insects, there are lots of birds. Flocks of starlings dive-bomb the fields. Swallows come like gray smoke from the mountains and strafe the foothills. They skim along the water at dusk and scoop up prodigious numbers of insect larvae, gnats and mosquitos. Barn swallows build their nests in the eaves of the patio in the springtime and, when the offspring are mature enough, the adults teach them to fly in the garden.

There are small Sinaloan crows and large Chihuahuan ravens which eat the locusts and the worms, and caw raucously in the rain. Their antics are as close as you'll get to a cartoon version of "Singing In The Rain," with leaps and turns and flutters, as if their wings were black umbrellas glistening, and their gruff voices, rich baritones to be proud of.

There are yellow tanagers which live in the oak trees and eat the mites. Like trees of canaries, the oak stands are filled with color and music when the late afternoon sunlight fades behind the mountain and the madrone shines with a fiery light.

After the plowing (and sometimes during it), undeterred by the dust or the sounds of the tractor, pure white egrets come to the *ejido*. They are cattle egrets which eat the grubs, the corn worms and beetles. They perch on the backs of cows and horses and eat the ticks and the horseflies that had plagued the livestock in the months before. And there are doves.

There are also herons which stalk the fields like overseers, crossing from furrow to furrow on their great spindly legs. They are infrequent visitors and each time one sees them there is the electric shock of wonder that they should have come here of all places, like pelicans in the desert. And, as usual, there are doves.

There are kingfishers with their Bart Simpson hairdos and their rattling calls. Blue-crested and active, they disturb all the other birds around them. There are woodpeckers, too, with red crowns, and there are flycatchers. There is a marvelous winter guest called the Great Kiskadee who comes in his yellow insouciance and lords over all the non-predatory birds in the *ejido*.

Flirting amid the jasmine blossoms and the birds of paradise are ruby throated hummingbirds, bright and quick as summer lightning, glittering like shards of colored glass, they come and go, seen more often from the periphery of one's vision than head on. Sometimes, too, broad-billed hummingbirds come with glittering blue gorgets and dark green wings like bright clear messengers from an old Inca god. And, of course, there are doves.

Always in Mexico there are doves. Cooing and rooing, calling back and forth, mourning doves chorus each morning in the cool air; they call across the echoing hills in the warm dusk of sun-splashed days. Their round, mellifluous calls reverberate in an antiphony, catholic and pervasive, which say *this is Mexico!* Which tell you, no matter where you go from here, you will always be haunted; whether you believe it or not, some part of your morning will always long for their call; some part of your evening will never be complete until you return.

And because of these insects which Twain found so useless, so obvious a proof there was no loving Creator, we have in Jalisco the incessant pollination which brings the hundred varieties of roses in Guadalajara, the *rosa argosa* of Puerto Vallarta, the flame tree of Zapopan, the jacaranda of Tonala, the bougainvillea which covers the walls of rich estates and the peasant's stucco with the same indiscriminate beauty. Banana trees grow in the shade; plane trees, willows and cottonwoods flourish by the sides of streams, flowing or not. Bronzed cowbirds and meadowlarks and sparrows live in the palms, the ficus and the eucalyptus which grow abundantly in large cities and remote village alike.

There are white and pink *nochebuenas* as well as the ubiquitous red ones which are not little Christmas plants as are their transplanted U.S. counterparts (poinsettias), but lush bushes eight and ten feet high with a hundred blossoms. There are lemon trees and lime trees. Grapefruits, oranges, mangoes and other fruits too exotic to name in English which grow right in the backyard. There were fresh figs last summer, and right outside my bedroom window is an *aguacate* tree so heavy with ripe avocados that the branches droop to the ground.

Now, over the desiccated corn stalks, float a pair of hawks searching for rabbits, field mice, or other small animals which live there off the grain and the insects which the fields so richly provide. They glide on thermals without the slightest effort high above me. And, when one finally dives, it does so soundlessly, as the wings—folded for the least resistance—allow him to drop like a stone. Just before hitting the victim, his talons extended, the hawk utters a sharp cry, brakes sharply, and with all the terror of a natural *blitzkrieg* buries his claws deep and mortally in the soft back of his prey.

In the madrone trees to the west are whiskered screech owls which sing in duets at night. One begins with short, irregular hoots like Morse code and is joined by his mate like an echo. Sometimes they whistle on one pitch and at a fairly even tempo. Coyotes wail at the moon in the evening, too, and are joined by the neighboring dogs performing an impromptu symphony for that lump of rock men have walked on, which has no light of its own, but which moves the tides and our blood with its power, and has inspired the least worthy of us to poetry.

Always at night there are stars. Millions visible to the naked eye; billions more cloaked in what seems to be the milk of the Milky Way, a cloudy phosphorescence which extends to the rim of the horizon. There is no light pollution from the city. There are no lights of factories, nor street lamps, nor highway illumination. The sky forms a perfect canopy of black velvet on which the stars and planets (like those planetarium light shows) can be seen clearly: Orion, Belatrix, Betelgeuse, the blue throbbing of Venus, the red glow of Mars.

And when the moon is full, or sometimes just as dawn is appearing over the *ejido* and the doves have not yet awakened (the time between darkness and daylight Mexicans call *la madrugada*) a golden eagle descends from his aerie hidden high in the Sierra Madres. Watching him in the chill of the early morning, one stands awestruck and, regardless of theology and its abstractions, breathes a prayer of thanks to whatever force invested this creation.

Mark Twain is an American institution. He was a good writer and a fine social critic. But Twain was an indifferent naturalist and a poor poet. The qualities which make for poetry, I suspect, are also those which make for a deeply alive human being. It requires a sense of wonder, a willingness to submerge the petty ego in the larger life of which man is but a part. One loses something ineffable but valuable if one is so full of oneself that the world is seen simply as a backdrop to one's own career and comfort.

My landlady has her four grandchildren visiting her this weekend.

They are young children—one about four months, the others pre-kinder. Children at those ages are demanding and always present. If one can't stand being drooled on, peed on, or awakened at odd hours, then it is advisable not to have children. They can be far more annoying than the innocuous housefly. Be warned, however, if you choose not to be bothered, you will also miss their fleeting beauty, their ephemeral growth, the miracle of their learning, the wonder of their individualism, the magic of their lives which will enrich you and deepen you as a human being.

Similarly, if you don't like flying and crawling insects, stay away from this part of Mexico. Read your Mark Twain in your comfortable apartment and assume you have all the answers. But you will miss a part of creation which cannot be duplicated in the antiseptic, air-conditioned suburbs of the north. You will miss the lushness, the myriad complexity, the color and the beauty of a world which is never quite reducible to human terms: lovely, terrible, elusive. Much like our children, the richness of these fields is never ours alone. They and it will continue long after we are gone. Today, even as they deepen our lives, holding—as the swallows do—both the sunlight and the air—they also remind us of our mortality, the bright smoke of wings in the sky.

THE BUS FROM HELL, or
GOING TO SEE FIDEL

The Iberoamerican Summit Conference is to take place in Guadalajara today. The presidents from all the South and Central American nations will be here along with the Prime Minister of Portugal, the King of Spain, and (are you ready for this?) Fidel Castro. That's right, Fidel himself. The meeting is to be at the Instituto Cabañas, and I am headed down to El Centro where I hope to catch a glimpse of him on his way in. Lucinda has demurred. She thinks that the crowds (estimated conservatively at 800,000) will be overwhelming, and that there will be so much security one won't be able to get within shouting distance of Castro himself. She's probably right but it's worth a try.

Castro is quite popular here among the Mexicans and is highly respected by the government. He has had a long-standing friendship with the country. He came here after his first failed attempt to overthrow Batista, and here was where he planned the successful revolution. In later years, when the U.S. and most of South America turned against Castro, Mexico stayed loyal, supporting his lone nay votes in the U.N., providing technical assistance, and maintaining diplomatic relations despite heavy pressures from the North.

He is certainly one of the most colorful of the world's leaders: charismatic, a dynamic speaker, forceful, and… perennial. But there are other reasons I'm going to see him today. Or at least try.

Born on Bastille Day and raised by an Irish grandfather who took part in the 1916 Uprising in Dublin, I have a special affinity for revolutionaries, especially those who threw off an obvious tyranny. And the month of July is a time when we remember some of the greatest. July 4, 1776. July 14, 1789. July 26, 1953. The last one is not very popular in revisionist U.S. history books these days, but it is indelible in my memory.

Fulgencio Batista was a typical strongman who took control of Cuba in a 1938 political coup when he was army chief of staff. He was elected president in 1940 and then was defeated for re-election in 1944. Disgruntled by the workings of democracy in 1952 he seized power, and later had himself "elected" president. His rule was blatantly corrupt and Cuba was a police state during his reign. He surrounded himself with venal officials who took payoffs from American gamblers running the Havana casinos, demanded bribes from Cubans for public services, and enriched themselves at public expense. Those who protested were murdered and their bodies were dropped in gutters as a warning. But Batista kept Havana a pleasure palace for rich Americans: popular night clubs and lavish shows, spiced by legalized gambling and prostitution. He also protected the exploitive American Fruit Company's lands, U.S. sugar interests, and our military bases on Guantanamo. So, during the Eisenhower Administration we provided Batista with sufficient arms to keep his island paradise well-guarded, the people suppressed, and business-as-usual.

Fidel Castro Ruz, a young attorney, angered by this corruption, the prostitution of Cuban women, and the degradation of his people, unsuccessfully attacked an army post on July 26, 1953 with a small group of men in an attempt to initiate a revolt. The attempt failed and Castro was imprisoned for a time and then released. In 1955 he went to Mexico where he organized the 26th of July Movement. On Christmas Day

1956, with nine others including his brother Raul and Ernesto "Che" Guevara (an Argentine physician), he returned to Cuba, evaded Batista's troops, and set up guerilla headquarters in the rugged hills of the Sierra Maestra. By 1958 his force had grown to 2,000 men and women. The rebels attacked and routed 3,000 government troops and took Santa Clara, 150 miles from Havana. A trainload of Batista reinforcements sent up the following day refused to get off the train and fight. It was the beginning of the end. As the Castro forces grew more powerful and more popular, the U.S. cut off arms shipments to Batista. On New Year's Day 1959, Batista flew to exile in the Dominican Republic, and Castro took power.

The people of the United States cheered this great victory. In 1959, Fidel Castro was considered by almost everybody a genuine hero. The U.S. Government, though slow to act in his support, thought that Castro would act in accord with U.S. interests. It was to become quickly disenchanted. Castro kicked out the gamblers, closed down the casinos and whorehouses, and replaced them with schools and hospitals. He also confiscated U.S. investments in banks, seized corporate landholdings and nationalized local industries. He began collective farming, moved the country inexorably into a socialist state, and indicated that he would accept aid from any nation, socialistic or capitalistic, which did not interfere with his internal affairs. The U.S. broke diplomatic relations with Cuba on January 3, 1961. Castro then forged an alliance with the Soviet Union.

During the last days of the Eisenhower Administration the CIA recruited and organized Cuban exiles in Florida into a Cuban Invasionary Force. When Kennedy took office, he made the ill-advised decision to proceed with an actual invasion of Cuba by this group. On April 17, 1961, he gave the order for the invasion but without U.S. air support. This, and the fact that the invaders did not receive the expected help from an anxious-to-be-liberated populace, insured that the

Bay of Pigs invasion would be easily crushed by Castro's forces. U.S.-Cuban relations have deteriorated significantly since then: the Soviet missile sites, the Quarantine, the Blockade by Kennedy, the exodus of the Mariel undesirables, various assassination attempts on Castro by the CIA and, finally, the listing by President Reagan of Cuba as a terrorist state.

Mistakes have been made throughout the long and ugly history of U.S.-Cuban relations, and this is not a brief for either side. The fact remains that Castro himself is and has been one of the most charismatic revolutionary figures in the world. He is a man of proven courage, sagacity and will. He is an underdog in a world run by superpowers who have not managed to bring him to heel or weaken his resolve. For four decades against great odds he has managed to stay in power and hold his country together while continuing to provide a consistent dissenting voice in world councils.

I park my car on a side street and walk down to Avenida Hidalgo, a four-lane shady avenue divided by a grassy tree-lined center strip. There are police (both local *transitos* and *camino federales*) every hundred feet. Small groups of people are lined up as far as I can see on both sides of the avenue. I stop and speak to a young father standing with his two daughters:

"*¿Ha visto a Fidel?*"

"*No, solamente a Sra. Chamorra. Pero, Fidel es lo que venimos a ver.*"

I'm in luck. He hasn't passed this way yet. I was also right in my supposition that Fidel is the one whom most of the Mexicans have turned out to see.

I begin walking down Hidalgo, hoping to catch one of the *par vials*, or electric buses, which go downtown. But it becomes apparent as I walk that they are not running today. I cross over to the center strip as the delegation from Chile passes by. The *transito*, a sergeant in a well-pressed blue uniform, comes over to where I am standing.

"Why do you stand here?" he asks.

"I want to see Fidel when he passes," I answer.

"I thought you Americans didn't like Fidel," he says.

"Some Americans," I answer. But it is, as we know, more complicated than that.

Then suddenly, I see the odd red, white and blue flag with the lone
star in its flat geometry coming down the road. A Chevrolet suburban
with a large white sign on the windshield reading "Cuba" confirms that
this is Castro's party. The blue van is packed with what appear to be
security people. Behind them are two Mexican motorcycle police, and
already I can hear the cheers of the crowd. And then, in a sedate Lin-
coln town car, there is Fidel, dressed as always in his uniform of olive
green with red/gold epaulets and a major's insignia on the collar. While
there are generals in Cuba, the revolutionary Comandante holds the
highest rank. Above the four brass buttons of his tunic is a full, gray
beard. He looks like the picture of Walt Whitman from the American
Lit. text! His eyes sparkle; he waves his hand to me in a half salute and
is gone.

It's hard to describe what I feel at this moment. I was sixteen years
old when Castro came to power. I remember his victory speeches on
American t.v., his trip to New York, and the people in Times Square
according him a hero's welcome. I remember the thrill of having a genuine and popular revolution in my generation. My Irish grandfather,
who had talked to me so often of the Easter Monday Rebellion of 1916,
joined me in cheering this new leader who overcame great odds to lead
his people against tyranny and who managed, unlike Padraic Pearse,
not to have his neck stretched at the end of a noose for his heroism.

Now, more than forty years later, in a world where most of the real
heroes are either dead or debunked, here he was not ten feet away from
me. Sixty-five years old and, except for the beard, you might easily have
guessed forty. A barrel-chested man with an aura of vitality and power

which was palpable, and in the eyes a pleasantness, a genuine aspect of good-natured modesty, as if to say: "All this pomp for such a bunch of old windbags!" I felt an electric rush comparable to nothing I can remember, not even the day I met John F. Kennedy at Boston College in 1963.

I would like to go down to the Instituto Cabañas but there are no cars on the street, no taxis, no buses running. The day is hot and humid. It is almost 2 p.m. and the summit meeting will have started by the time I walked to the central part of town. Just as I'm about to turn back, however, a dilapidated white bus spewing exhaust comes barreling down the street. On the windshield written in black grease pencil it reads: "Ruta 400. Arcos/Centro." Behind the wheel is a middle-aged dark-skinned Mexican with wild eyes. I wave to him. In a teeth-rattling screech of brakes he pulls to a stop twenty feet away. I quickly board and give him the fare.

"*¿Al centro?*" I ask.

"*¿Sí, cómo no?*" he replies.

Why not indeed. Except that there are dozens of cops lining both sides of the avenue now. There are roadblocks in front of every side street. This bus getting to the *Centro* is about as likely as a person selling Chiclets getting into the presidential palace to make a sale in the middle of the night.

At each intersection there are *federales* waving frantically, and soldiers with machine guns on every corner. We fly down the *avenida* in a clash of gears. The bus is mostly empty. I look at a couple of other passengers and they shrug. We all resume staring out the window.

Now there is the sound of sirens and motorcycles behind us as the delegation from Venezuela passes us and there are cheers, flags waving, and people shouting. We pass the intersection of Avenida Unión through more roadblocks, army trucks and policeman who are waving frantically. Here the crowds line the street three and four deep. There are thousands of people out to see the dignitaries pass. It is a great day in Guadalajara. More sirens and motorcycles and the Uruguay delegation passes us.

Now we come to the grand intersection of Federalismo and Hidalgo, and the crowds here are eight and ten deep, well over twenty thousand. The police and soldiers are trying to hold them back as they edge out into the street to see who the next delegation could be. A roar goes up from the crowd. What can it be? And now I see from the window that it is *us* they are cheering. They smile, they wave, they clap their hands. The Bus From Hell barreling along at forty miles an hour, going through roadblocks, past blue uniforms, brown uniforms, *tránsitos, federales,* soldiers with black machine guns.

"*¡ORALE!*" the crowd screams.

"*¡BIEN HECHO, VIEJO!*"

"*¡QUE PADRE!*"

Young men, street vendors, school girls, mothers with babies, businessmen, all laughing and cheering as we proceed down the main thoroughfare behind presidents, prime ministers, a hero, and a king.

"GREAT WORK, OLD MAN. BEAUTIFUL!"

And the driver nods his head, acknowledging the crowd as if it is no more than his due.

There is something in the Mexican character which is definitely attracted by the anarchistic impulse. I have seen this happen twice before. Once when a soldier was ordering people off the tarmac at an air show and was thrusting his gun in people's faces. It was a tense uncomfortable situation. A little girl went up to the soldier and said simply, "*¡Hola!*" and the soldier, a boy of about nineteen, lost his composure and the crowd all laughed and the soldier joined them in good-natured laughter at his own expense. Another time was when a roadblock had been set up to clear some lightning-struck trees from the road. A crowd gathered and cheered everyone who defied the cops and the barrier to go on through—much like they were cheering now for our bus. But it was a much smaller crowd then and a much less serious situation.

This is quite different. Here we have the leaders of all the South American, Central American and Caribbean countries, many of them with their own security. Plus the King of Spain for godsakes. And, as anyone can see at this point, there are soldiers on rooftops, armored vehicles, hundreds of not-very-friendly-looking *federales*, and secret service men not in uniform.

Ultimately, two blocks from the underground garage where the dignitaries have gone, a police car forces us down a side street where we disembark. There are about ten of us on board and it has been the ride of a lifetime. We thank the driver and, while most of the passengers take off, I stay around to see what will happen. One policeman (smiling!) gets out of his car and comes over. He tells the driver to get the damn bus out of there. And the driver pulls away smiling in a cloud of exhaust.

I couldn't help thinking what might have happened to that bus driver outside of Mexico. In the U.S. he surely would have been handcuffed and carted off to jail. Probably charged with one or more federal offenses. Endangering a presidential party. Jeopardizing the safety of diplomatic personnel. In some countries snipers would have disabled the bus, shot the driver, and then the government would have interned and interrogated the passengers for hours or even days. But here in Mexico they let the driver go. He had merely punctured the pomposity of a parade to a summit meeting and that's no crime. He gave us a reminder that all people, bus riders and presidents, are human beings.

I'd like to think that he also reminded us that a Mexican bus driver with *cojones* is something worth cheering about in this pusillanimous age, and that you don't have to wear the uniform of Comandante to be a genuine hero.

THE BLIND MEN OF INDOSTAN

The school has finally sent a couple of men to install the light fixtures in our house. They are affable and competent and go right to work without preliminaries. I put on a tape by the Tigres del Norte to give them music to work by while Lucinda brews a pot of coffee. Jesús, slim but solid, with a fierce Villa moustache and an amused glint in his eye, makes jokes from time to time. He speaks no English and has the complexion of buffed mahogany. His assistant, a heavy-set youngster named Luís, laughs appreciatively at the jokes and occasionally asks in Spanish where a particular electrical outlet is, or whether we have more light bulbs.

Fresh coffee is brewing so I ask them both if they would like a cup. Luís declines politely. Jesús says something in Spanish with a smile which has the words *agua* and *prieta* in it. I attempt a translation for Lucinda.

"I think he said that he doesn't drink coffee because it is merely dark water to him."

Mildly annoyed, Lucinda replies, "No, no. What I think he said was that *he* was dark."

"Well, of course he is, but it hardly makes sense to say that when someone offers you coffee!"

"I know, I know. But I think he was making some kind of complicated joke. A pun maybe."

"Well, that's what I *said*. Coffee is like dark water."

"But that's not what I heard. It was different."

Meanwhile Luís, who we now discover speaks some English, is over in the corner clipping some wires together and chuckling at our dispute.

"¿*Que significa*?" I ask.

Still smiling he tells us. "What Jesús says was that he's very brown already, so he has to watch out because drinking the dark water of coffee could make him even browner."

"Ah, *éso* !" We join good-naturedly in the laughter as he translates our misunderstanding to Jesús.

I am reminded of the narrative poem called "The Blind Men of Indostan" which I learned as a child. It tells, you might remember, of six blind men who encounter an elephant. The first blind man, feeling the beast's side, says, "It is very like a wall." The second, feeling the tusk of the elephant, says, "It is very like a spear." The third, taking the squirming trunk in his hands observes that "It is very like a snake." The fourth feels the elephant's knee and says, "It is very like a tree." The fifth says (feeling the ear), "Even the blindest man can see it's very like a fan." The sixth seizes the swinging tail and says, "It is very like a rope." The story ends:

And so these men of Indostan
Disputed loud and long
Each in his own opinion
Exceeding stiff and strong,
Though each was partly in the right
And all were in the wrong.

And so that's us today. Lucinda reminds me of the time we were both riding the BART train in San Francisco and two elderly Vietnamese women were talking about their destination. The first lady said that they needed to get off at "FORASH ILL." The second replied that no, the station was pronounced "FROEET ILLA." And she looked quite smug about this fact. She smiled proudly when I caught her eye, one good English speaker confirming another. The first lady meekly accepted her friend's superior pronunciation.

I had no idea what they were talking about until they both got up at the FOREST HILLS stop and the second old lady turned to me with a triumphant grin: FROEET ILLA! Of course.

Events like these, which were cause for amusement then, are now appropriate reminders of just how foolish it is to be smug about whatever knowledge we may *think* we have.

Our friend the poet Richard Shelton relates one of his "classic blunders" in Spanish in his wonderful book *Going Back To Bisbee*.

> Although it was one of many, it stands out in my mind. I had just arrived in Cuernavaca after a three-day train and bus ride from Nogales. I was exhausted and sick. The taxi driver deposited me and my luggage in front of the house where I had rented a room from a Mexican family. My landlady-to-be, a truly gracious person, came out to the sidewalk to meet me and escort me in. Looking at my haggard face, she asked me in Spanish, "Are you tired?" The word is *cansado*. But I confused it with *casado* (married) and in my impeccable Spanish replied, "Yes, I have been tired for fifteen years and I have a twelve-year-old son." Her eyes opened wider for a moment, but she merely nodded, patted me on the shoulder with compassion, and led me into the house to rest after my long ordeal.

Our Spanish had much improved, though, after the first two years in Guadalajara. Usually we got the import of what was being said and could figure out the words we didn't know from the context. If we couldn't, we'd ask for a clarification. There were exceptions, of course. Sometimes the same word can mean different things. For example, *aguas* ("waters" and "Watch out!") or *escaleras* ("stairs" and "stepladder"), our second point of confusion on this particular morning. We were grateful for having the error pointed out and usually could laugh about it.

In reading a contemporary short story, however, it is quite possible to understand almost the entire piece and then completely lose the import of the story on the last page because the meaning is suggested subtly rather than explicitly stated, or because the language becomes rhetorical. For example, in "*El Taxista*," a story we read for our Spanish class, he either killed his wife at the end, or he put her in a taxi and sent her to her mother. Or she went to her mother's in a taxi and killed herself. Or, nobody died but she would have liked to have killed: (a) herself, (b) the taxi driver, (c) her mother.

"Did we all read the same story?" asked *la profesora,* when we reviewed the material in class the next day.

Meanwhile, Jesús is asking if he can use the stairs. I am about to point out the obvious—we live in a one-story house—when Lucinda subtly nods to the stepladder in the corner of the kitchen.

"*¿Cómo no?* I reply. "Yes, of course." Grateful to be *cansado,* especially when I am so *casado.*

THE GREAT KISKADEE

On the other side of the brick wall that surrounds our garden is an *ejido*, which at this time of year is bright green and gold with tasseled corn stalks. There is the occasional snort of the foreman's horse; the bray of a burro staked near a flimsy hut. The air is alive with the flashing wings of barn swallows diving for insects in the water trough. The call of doves echoes across the hills.

It is deep in the rainy season, but today it is warm and dry. It is Saturday and no one is working in the fields. It is so quiet I can hear the crunch of a horse tearing up clumps of grass three hundred feet away. Barn swallows flash in and out of the eaves under the porch. The fig tree is heavy with ripe fruit; the *aguacates*, too, are softening their hard green dimples into an edible black. The banana tree hangs heavy, testicle-like, with seed pod and ripe fruit.

I have almost nodded asleep over papers that I have been correcting since noon when I hear a piercing: KREEE! KREEE! The sound is coming from deep in the foliage of the banana tree. Its heavy green and yellow leaves waxily conceal whatever avian stranger has arrived on the patio. Then the tree branches shake, the leaves rustle ominously. Other birds have already flown off as if scattered by a hawk. Except for the arrogant rustle in the banana tree, everything around has gone silent. The doves no longer call in the hills. The swallows have disappeared. Even the horse has ceased his cropping of the grass on the other side of the wall.

Perhaps this is not a bird at all, as I first thought. Perhaps it is some kind of animal. A squirrel, a raccoon, a skunk, a wildcat from the dark Bosque de La Primavera just the other side of the tilled land? I approach the tree cautiously. KREEE! KREEE! The high-pitched screech again. Then, a flash of yellow and it is gone.

I go back to correcting papers written by high school juniors on the development of the North American colonies. "Southerners were too lazy to work," writes one student. "That's why they imported slaves." Hmm. If they were too lazy to work, why make the arduous trip across the Atlantic, why work like oxen to plow the land, why establish a plantation in the first place? There are more comfortable ways to live than as a colonist in a new, unfriendly, and uncleared land. It is a bit more complicated than that. And more interesting. Like life. Like the flash of yellow seen in the banana tree. It requires patience; waiting until more facts are available before coming to a decision. It requires taking the time to find more pieces of the puzzle, and then slowly and without prejudice putting the pieces of the puzzle together. Earlier traditions called this "scholarship."

We often settle for easy answers because *we're* lazy. Ascribing those qualities to Southerners was, I suspect, projection on the part of the student.

While I am thinking this, I hear the harsh KREEE! again. I look over my shoulder and this time catch a glimpse of the bird before he flies away again. About the size of a crow. He has a bright yellow chest, and a sharply patterned black and white head.

His head is like that of a jay, and so are his mannerisms. Aggressive, intrusive, frightening other birds away, noisy, quarrelsome. Yet, I know there is no such thing as a yellow jay. The Mexican jay is dull blue with brown on the back. Its call is *zwink, zwink*. The Steller jay is often found down here, too. But it is blue and black with wings, tail, and belly deep blue. You see them in the Western U.S., mostly, especially around campgrounds. They are camp thieves, as a matter of fact, and will take your wristwatch as quickly as your morning biscuits. Querulous, forward, noisy. But not yellow in spirit or in color. And their call is *shack, shack, shack.*

Maybe it is some kind of parrot, either escaped from a nearby house or (unlikely) migrated north from the jungles of Chiapas or Guatemala. I write down his markings in my notebook and then go into the house to check the *Peterson Field Guide.* I start looking for yellow birds: orioles, tanagers, finches, warblers, vireos, cuckoos. Cuckoos? I'm going cuckoo. Never realized how many yellow birds there were in Mexico. And all of these are too small.

Let's see. Woodpecker. Hmm. Has similar marks on the head but no yellow on the breast. Trogon. Yellow breast but no black and white marks on the head. Kingbird. Almost, but the markings on the head are absent here, too. Flycatcher! Same size? Yep. Black and white stripes on the head. *Sí.* Yellow breast? Yes. "Wings a dull brown." Hmm. Not sure; can't remember the exact color of the wings; it moved so quickly. "The Boat-billed Flycatcher." That's probably it. Voice. "A rough, rasping KEE'RICK." Hmm. Rough and rasping all right, but the call I heard was only one syllable. And I think I remember the wings as being more of a russet shade than dull brown.

I return to the patio. It is late afternoon and the brick wall holds all the heat of the day like a reflector oven. The pale orange hibiscus has begun to close its blossoms. The palms throw low shadows against the house. Suddenly, KREEE! The visitor returneth. Like Poe's raven, his appearances have been sudden and peremptory. *Not the least obeisance made he; not a minute stopped or stayed he.*

Now he is poised just above the patio wall. The barn swallows have flitted away in panic. My ungracious visitor swoops from the wall to the top of the palm tree and sits there watching *me.* KREEE! The voice *is* one syllable. The wings *are* russet. He seizes a red caterpillar. *Jeep-jeep purrr* is the sound he makes now as he devours the insect.

He flies to the top of the banana tree and sits there poised, king of the world, looking down at me. As if for all the world he were posing. As if he were saying: *Don't sell me short. I'm no ordinary bird.* Or maybe, *Double check that book of yours, teacher. I'm far more interesting than you think.*

I return to *Peterson's Field Guide.* "Bright yellow underparts, strikingly patterned black and white head is common to Boat-billed and Social flycatchers. Note: bright rufous in wings and tail are absent in these species. The flycatcher with rufous [or russet!] wings is… THE GREAT KISKADEE. See p. 144." Turning the page quickly… "KISKADEE. Voice: a loud *DZEEE* or *QUEEE.* [Close enough to my *KREEE*] Also *Geep-geep career.*" [And *that's* close enough to my *Jeep-jeep purrr.*]

Ha! *Eso es!* "Habitat: MEXICO. Sonora-south. Pacific coast to central plateau. Sea level to 6,000 feet. Woodland borders, plantations…"

Plantations! Back to them again. Lazy Southerners and plantations. Lazy Mexicans, some Anglos think, and underproductive *ejidos.* How easy it is to mislabel though lack of knowledge. To not know the vagaries of landscape and the problems of water, and call Mexicans underproductive. To not know the russet wings of the Great Kiskadee and call him a Boat-billed flycatcher. To not know Jefferson, the last of the Renaissance men, or Madison, the workhorse of the Constitution, and call Southerners lazy.

This past summer I returned to Newport, Rhode Island, to visit my mother. I also travelled to Boston and walked the Freedom Trail, spent some hours in the Widener Library at Harvard, passed a pleasant pair of hours in the house and garden of Longfellow, and ambled along the tree-lined streets of Cambridge.

For me, the return to New England was also a return to my roots after a long absence. I had an opportunity to re-acquaint myself with the history of that small pocket of the world which was to so drastically change history. The fact that I was to teach the Colonial Period in American Literature in the coming semester was an incentive to re-acquaint myself with the history and early culture of the area. I don't think I've ever had a more productive summer.

The student paper I am reading now says: "Perhaps the greatest contribution of Calvinism was how it created a belief that to labor industriously was one of God's commands. It resulted in general prosperity in New England, the 'work ethic,' and a belief that success in any endeavor was a mark of God's favor."

Slowly and carefully (I am, after all, an *Irish-Catholic* teaching in Mexico) I set aside the blue pen I have been using for this journal. I pick up a red one and, with a deeply contented sigh, write a capital A at the top of the paper. The GREAT KISKADEE strikes again.

PERMISSION TO SPEAK

As a child I had a terrible stammer which worsened as adolescence came with its hormonal stresses and changes. I could not pronounce a vowel without a machine gun stutter of repetition. "Aa-aa-aa-apple," I would say. "Or-or-or-orange," I would splutter. In anticipation of such problems I had learned to glue articles or adjectives to such words so that a consonant would preface each noun. "Give me th'apple," I'd say or "N'orange, please." All this planning went out the window, however, in times of emotional excitement when, through enthusiasm or anger, the words flowed faster than my deliberation could arrange them.

This weakness, this flaw, had its compensations at times. In the effort to find adjectives, to rearrange sentences, I developed a facility with language and a skill at rearranging words. All my comments were second draft and thus when I did finally speak, my words often had a deliberation and weight to them which they retain today. My wife observes that I seem to invest a simple comment about taking out the garbage with all the high seriousness of a declamation on the vagaries of the Supreme Court. As a poet, the discipline of trying differing combinations of words and syllables is, as a result of this early practice, deeply ingrained.

Yet, at the age of fourteen, stammering was a painful and embarrassing infirmity. A bright child, I was often faced with the dilemma in class of not answering a question I knew for fear of making an embarrassing spectacle of myself, or answering the question after taking pains in word order and placement of consonants only to find to my chagrin that there was a follow-up question I had not anticipated. Here's a typical example of the second scenario:

"Can anyone tell us who was the most important Catholic philosopher? Yes, Michael?"

"That would be the philosopher, Thomas" (watch the **A** coming up), "ah… Thomas S'Aquinas. He was the" (change author for…) "writer who gave us the *Summa Theologica*."

"Very good, Michael. And what was the name of the Greek philosopher who influenced him?"

"Ah, ah, ah, eh, eh, eh, ay, aghr, Aristotle!"

I sat down to a chorus of laughs which obliterated my previous answer and relegated me to the position of class fool. Or worse: an object of pity to Mary Newbury, with whom I was desperately in love. I had not told her my feelings, of course, and my chances of declaring them and being taken seriously had vanished forever, I believed, after this latest exhibition.

One day, shortly after this episode, my ninth grade English teacher, Brother Felix, asked me to come see him after my last class. Our school, De La Salle Academy in Newport, Rhode Island, was run by the French Christian Brothers who had their rectory on school grounds. As a result, staying after school was not a hardship for the teachers. Essentially, they lived at school. Nevertheless, looking back now, except for the coaches and the most exigent of the disciplinarians, few hung around the school after the last bell.

Brother Felix was erasing the blackboard when I went in. He told me to have a seat and then he began telling me about his own school years. He told me that when he was a teenager he used to stutter but that he seldom did anymore. "How did you get over it?" I asked. He told me that essentially he used two tools which were readily available: singing and projecting the voice. "Do you like to sing?" he asked. I nodded. "And I'll bet you don't stutter when you sing; am I right?" I nodded again.

That week at his suggestion, I joined the school choir and began what would be a lifelong amateur passion for music. Even today, I sing at Irish gatherings on St. Patrick's Day, I sing Christmas carols each holiday season, I sing in church, and I sing with and to my own English classes at the school in Guadalajara where I teach. As a poet, I reach almost instinctively for the music of the line whether reading the works of another writer or composing my own.

At Brother Felix's suggestion, I practiced for Glee Club recitals, I sang solos in the school talent show, I sang high masses in the local Catholic Church, and I enriched my life in ways I could not have imagined then by studies of choral singing, Latin and French, and the history of music. I discovered the music of poetry in Virgil, in Eliot and in Octavio Paz much earlier and much more deeply than I uncovered the meaning.

The skills involved in projecting the voice were harder to learn. I began by shouting memorized speeches and poems to the back of the class where Brother Felix sat correcting papers, apparently indifferent to my efforts and focused on his grade book. At the end of the hour, though, he smiled, and noted how many lines I had recited without a stammer. By my sophomore year under his tutelage I had learned gestures, dramatic pauses, voice modulation and breathing control. I had memorized dozens of poems, speeches and scenes from plays. I had even begun to write my own scripts and short declamations. By my junior year I had won speech contests across the state, had been in a nationally-televised debate tournament, and had given extemporaneous talks in competitions, at Toastmasters, in student legislatures and at the Model U.N. in New York.

I discovered that, for me, speaking to large audiences was no more stressful than answering a question in class had been, or asking Mary

Newbury for a date. The former I did now with greater frequency. The latter, on the occasion of our Junior Prom, and Mary accepted with the comment, "Why did you take so long? I liked you when we were in the 9th grade!"

I discovered that focusing on a weakness with determination and diligence could turn that flaw into a strength. Speaking to my graduation class at commencement exercises, I received applause, not laughter or embarrassed silence. Much of it was due to the intervention of a caring and dedicated teacher.

Brother Felix, long since passed away, is part of who I am and hope to be today. He is with me when I give a poetry reading at the Three Rivers Arts Festival in Pittsburgh or at the Tequendama Inter-Continental in Bogotá, Colombia. He is with me as I work with my creative writing seminar or my American literature class, sharing the passion of writing and the beauty of literature with my Mexican students. I will never forget what he gave me on those schoolbound afternoons, and I try to emulate his example through my own mission as a teacher and as a poet. He gave me far more than a tool for dealing with a handicap. He gave me a key to the secret of living fully.

I am still a stammerer, of course. I have simply discovered a method wherein I manage to avoid stuttering most of the time, but always the tendency is there. Michael, the 9th grade student, is forever a part of who I am. When I am sufficiently moved by the language, or by an emotion, a click ascends in the larynx that sometimes is converted into a lilt, a thoughtful pause, a Kennedyesque repetition, or a doubling of the consonant. Other times, a dramatic turn in thought or image occurs, as I move to replace one word with another less troubling to the tongue.

For most of those who hear me speak, these devices are unremarked, or noticed simply as a wide range of rhetorical devices used by a speaker comfortable with language and ideas. Yet for Michael, the boy in the front row with his hand up, dreading what will come out of his mouth, they are the tools which made him a teacher and a poet. For Michael, the boy in the empty classroom declaiming Patrick Henry's "Give Me Liberty or Give Me Death," the boy in the choir transcendent with music, they are and always will be the stuff of miracles.

THROUGH US THE UNIVERSE TALKS TO ITSELF: THE POETRY OF OCTAVIO PAZ

When Octavio Paz died at the age of 84, he left behind a prodigious body of work in several genres: biography, literary criticism, social commentary, political analysis, and poetry. Most of the articles and memorials following the death of this Nobel laureate have focused on his political life and his contributions as a social critic. Yet, his vocation was, and he considered himself primarily to be, a poet.

Paz began publishing poetry at the age of seventeen, and in Mexico City founded with a group of friends what would be the first of many literary magazines. At the age of nineteen he published his first book of verse, *Luna Silvestre* (Savage Moon). He was to continue this prolific outpouring of language up until the time of his death, despite a full-time and active career as a diplomat working for 23 years as Mexican consular official in Paris, New York, San Francisco, Geneva, and as Mexican Ambassador to India. He began a second career in 1968, after resigning his post as ambassador in protest over the massacre of student demonstrators in Mexico City just prior to the Olympic Games held there that year. Subsequently, he went on to work as professor of literature at Cambridge, the University of Texas, Harvard, and U.C. Berkeley. In 1976 he founded *Vuelta*, which is still regarded as one of the most prestigious magazines in Latin America.

In the U.S. Paz is best known for his book *The Labyrinth of Soli-*

tude, which analyzes with brutal frankness the Mexican character, revealing among other things the tendency of Mexicans to wear masks, or to cover up their true emotions by assuming either a stoic indifference or a fiesta (*hasta mañana*) mentality. His famous analysis of the verb "*chingar*" (to screw, to rape) is a tour de force. He dates the word's origin from the invasion of the conquistadors and the virtual rape of the indigenous people by the Spaniards. Thus, according to Paz, Mexicans are "*hijos de la chingada,*" or children of the raped one. A big shot is a "*chingón,*" one who screws others. A useless thing is a "*chingadera,*" and the expression to hell with it, or, screw it, is "*a la chingada.*" Mexican speech is often peppered with variants of this verb, and the digression in this major work on Mexican culture is typical of Paz, whose first love always was language. He was fascinated with how language illustrates (even when we least intend it) who we truly are. Some called the book insightful, others railed against it. Yet, it got the world's attention and many believe it captured the Mexican personality with telling insight and humor.

In 1990, when Paz received the Nobel Prize for Literature, his poetry was not particularly well-known even in his own country, outside of a small circle of intellectuals. In the U.S., Muriel Rukeyser had translated his *Early Poems* (New Directions, 1973) and Denise Levertov and Lysander Camp had translated some shorter works. More significantly, Eliot Weinburger and New Directions had brought out *The Collected Poems 1957-1987* and it was in its second printing. Yet, if one were to ask the average reader of poetry either in Mexico or the United States to name a title of one of his books or poems, or even comment on Paz's antecedents or his contribution to literature, few responses would be forthcoming.

I had gone to teach in Guadalajara in the summer of 1989 and was amazed to discover that his work was not taught there as part of any literature curriculum, and that many professors of literature, while familiar with his essays, found his poetry to be "oblique" or "inaccessible." I spent the next year preparing a Paz seminar which I now conduct annually and, in the process, discovered that much of his work is as accessible as Frost or Stafford. His "obliqueness" is merely an abandonment in mid-phrase of the narrative for an image—a technique that Eliot often uses in the *Four Quartets*. Image, of course, is central to Paz. Take this delightful example:

> Stillness
>   not on the branch
> in the air
>   not in the air
> in the moment
>   hummingbird.

("La Exclamación")

The oxymoron of the still moment (or the moving stillness), the shaped verse, the impact of the surface simplicity but "mot juste" exactitude, is characteristic of Paz. As is the leap or transcendental moment which is captured by the poet's close observation and the Oriental brush stokes of language. His debt to the Imagists and to Pound might also be seen in some of his short poems.

One of my students compared the poem quoted above to Pound's "In The Metro" in a critical paper. ("The apparition of these faces in the crowd/Petals on a wet, black bough.") The student was a careful scholar of American literature and his instincts were correct. At the age of 30 Paz had received a Guggenheim fellowship and gone to New York where he studied the work of Ezra Pound, as well as that of T.S. Eliot, William Carlos Williams and Wallace Stevens. His debt to Pound and, as we shall later see, to Eliot is significant.

Paz's life and his political change from the enthusiasm of communist fellow traveller in the 1930s to conservative acrimony of a disappointed idealist in the 1960s (which expressed itself in criticism of both

Fidel Castro and the Sandinistas of Nicaragua) has been the focus of many of the articles written about him since his death. In Mexico, his protest against his own government for the student massacre of 1968 has been resurrected at length in newspapers and magazines, as has the debate about whether he justly appraised his fellow countrymen in *Labyrinth of Solitude.* This type of popular political biography, I suppose, is to be expected when a poet has become something of an international celebrity. However, it is disturbing when magazines devoted to poetry and its practice succumb to this media reductionism. After all, Paz did receive the Nobel Prize for literature, not for sociology or political science.

An issue of *Poets & Writers Magazine,* to cite one example, which appeared shortly after his death, carried a lead story about Paz. Written by Alberto Rios, Regents' Professor of English at Arizona State University, it did little to enlighten the readers (whom we might assume to be poets and writers themselves) as to the substance of Paz's poetry. There are the same biographical highlights released by the UPI, the political intricacies of his life, and an anecdote about the author's frustrated attempt to meet Paz in Mexico. This is unfortunate. We need to demand more as poets and writers (or as readers of *Poets & Writers*) than personality. Paz himself, an Eliot scholar, would have remembered the words from "Tradition and the Individual Talent" where Eliot wrote: "The progress of an artist is a continual self-sacrifice, a continual extinction of personality... No poet, no artist of any art, has his complete meaning alone. His significance, his appreciation is the appreciation of his relation to dead poets and artists. You cannot value him alone; you must set him, for contrast and comparison, among the dead." Alberto Rios, himself a poet with an international reputation, surely must have felt the pull and tug of these lines:

> others
> are always others and are the same

they enter and expel us from ourselves
they see with our eyes what eyes do not see
There is another time within
time
still
with no hours no weight no shadow
without past or future
            only alive
like the old man on the bench
indivisible identical perpetual.
We never see it
            It is transparency.

It is in fact this transparency which forms the leitmotif of Paz's work. A friend of Paul Eluard, the French surrealist, he even stole his most famous line (an Eliot trick) and included it in a poem. "There is another world," Eluard wrote, "and it's in this one." "There is another world," Paz wrote, "in this one." Much of his poetry is an attempt to capture the penetration of this other world at the moment it appears in this one, that moment of "the timeless in time." It is an attempt to capture the light in the trees, the fire in the water or, as Eliot put it, "the music heard so deeply that it is not heard at all but you are the music while the music lasts." His debt to T.S. Eliot is real. Listen again to the voice of Paz:

Not the marvellous presented
                but the present sensed...
Not the same hours
                others
are always others and are the same
they enter and expel us from ourselves
they see with our eyes what our eyes do not see
There is another time within time
still
    with no hour no weight no shadow
without past or future
                only alive

like the old man on the bench
indivisible identical perpetual
We never see it
          It is transparency.
                    (from Paz's "*El Mismo Tiempo*")

Not the stillness of the violin while the note lasts
Not that only, but the coexistence,
Or say that the end precedes the beginning,
and the end and the beginning were always there
Before the beginning and after the end...
Time past and time future
are both contained in time present...
And all is always now.
You cannot face it steadily, but one thing is sure
That time is no healer...
The gift half guessed, the gift half understood, is Incarnation.
                    (from Eliot's *The Four Quartets*)

The Four Quartets has been referred to by Richard Shelton as "a magnificent failure." It was an attempt to weld a series of religious and philosphical ideas into an eclectic world view made intelligible only through images, or as T.S. Eliot would have it, by "objective correlatives." Eliot himself doubted whether he had been wholly successful. He wrote that "one has only learnt to get the better of words/For the thing one no longer has to say, or the way in which/One is no longer disposed to say it." And yet, any attempt to name the unnameable is destined to fail. "We had the experience but missed the meaning," Eliot tells us, and this hope to recover that meaning, to illuminate it in "hints and guesses, hints followed by guesses," is the leitmotif of *The Four Quartets*.

This is precisely what Wordsworth was trying for in "Tintern Abbey" (albeit in a more direct, even didactic, way) and in that evocative poem manages to illuminate transcendentalism in a way no lecture or essay by Ralph Waldo Emerson could do. So Paz with his "transparency" in "*El Mismo Tiempo*" and Eliot with his "Incarnation" in *The*

Four Quartets reach for spiritual truths which have been felt, deeply experienced (long before they were thought). The ambiguity which results in both their work comes from the difficulty of translating the ineffable into ideas and images which might form a meaningful matrix that the reader can experience.

Paz, like Eliot, absorbed philosophies and religions, taking what he needed from them to form his own eclectic intimation of the world. In his work we see transcendentalism, Buddhism, Zen, Hinduism and existentialism transformed in the caldron of personal experience and enlightment. While his Irish contemporary W.B. Yeats contended that the "center cannot hold," Paz continually sought the center, and gave it shape and substance, as in "*Concierto En El Jardín:*"

> It rained.
> The hour is an enormous eye.
> Inside it, we come and go like reflections.
> The river of music enters my blood.
> If I say *body*, it answers *wind*.
> If I say *earth*, it answers *where*.
>
> The world a double blossom, opens:
> sadness of having come
> joy of being here.
>
> I walk lost in my own center.

And again in the poem "Madrugada," he reached for the central core:

> Cold rapid hands
> draw back one by one
> the bandages of dark
> I open my eyes
>   still
> I am living
>   at the center
> of a wound still fresh.

Paz affirms in his work that the center does exist, is definable, and that it can indeed hold because it is transcendent of the self, whether through the incandescent moment in the garden (Eliot's "wild thyme unseen") or the torment of pain which forms that center, and unlike the self, it is eternal. Here again we see his debt not only to Eliot ("the point of intersection of the timeless with time") but also to Emerson, Wordsworth, even Li Po.

What is so delightful about introducing Mexican youngsters to his work, though, is their amazement when a poem hits upon a rich sensual vein. They have been told that Paz was an intellectual, a writer of poems which were not accessible, which yielded meaning only reluctantly to the initiated. Imagine their joy in reading these lines from "*Con Los Ojos Cerrados*:"

> With eyes closed
> you light up within
> you are a blind stone .
>
> Night after night I carve you
> with eyes closed
> you are frank stone
>
> we have become enormous
> just knowing each other
> with eyes closed.

One encounters few poems in any language which so powerfully present the intimacy of two lovers naked together and deeply in love. And yet the poem is as remarkable for its restraint as it is for its frank sexuality. It is as moving in its quiet way as the wonderful "Yes!" passage from Joyce's *Ulysses* or the passage when "the earth moves" in Hemingway's *For Whom The Bell Tolls*. Yet, it is more compact, more precise and more subtle without sacrificing any of the sensual impact.

One of the great failures of secondary education and even undergraduate education is that so few teachers will read or discuss contemporary poetry. Unable to trust their own judgment about what is good, not having a body of criticism or a critical text to quote from, many simply choose to ignore work which is moving, lyrical and relevant to their students. It is easier and safer to "analyze" Frost or e.e. cummings, describe how the Shakespearean sonnet is constructed, or talk about Emily Dickinson's feminism, than to grapple with the work of a contemporary. Besides, they say, most kids don't like poetry anyway.

My experience has been the opposite. My students love poetry and will even study meter and complex imagery as long as they're first allowed to hear the beauty of the work, and experience it first hand. My students at the American School in Guadalajara have not only heard and absorbed the sonnets of Shakespeare, but they've also come to appreciate the surrealism of Richard Shelton, the lyricism of Octavio Paz, the forthright New England iambs of Robert Frost, the subtle intricacies of Eliot and Pound, and the magic of Borges, Rilke, Jiménez, and Neruda. I never tell my students that a poet is esoteric, inaccesible, or difficult. I choose selections from the poet's work which sing to me; I present them with open affection, and in the process the students themselves come to appreciate, criticize, make comparisons, and ultimately incorporate in their own work and their own lives the beauty of the poetry.

And so back to Octavio Paz. I think this is what he would have wanted at the end of a life dedicated to creating images with words. Instead of the governmental eulogies (not believed by the students), the analyses of his political beliefs (relevant to them only in a peripheral sense as history), I think he would have preferred to know how the startling beauty of his poetry reached and snapped to attention the bored girl in the last row and made her sit up and pay attention with wonder at the magic of the language. And how there remained, when the poem was done, a sense of something greater than herself. A hint, a

guess at the infinite, which will enrich her life in maturity, in mother-
hood and in old age.

Niña

Between the afternoon, resisting,
and the night, gathering,
the gaze of a young girl

She abandons her notebooks and writing,
all of her being in two fixed eyes.
On the wall the light cancels itself.

Does she see her end or her beginning?
She'll say she sees nothing.
The infinite is transparent.

She'll never know what she saw.

MAME, DOUGHBOYS AND A.M.D.G.

I'll work backwards because I know how annoying abbreviations are to a reader. A.M.D.G. stands for *Ad Majorem Dei Gloriam*—For The Greater Glory of God. It was what the Jesuits wrote on the blackboard in class above the calculus equations or the list of Aristotle's elements of the tragic hero. Catholic school was like that when I was a kid. Knowledge and the difficulty of its acquisition were offered up like a cross. Later, as we copied the letters at the top of our composition or our final exam, they formed a simple prayer or forlorn hope for a passing grade.

These days I see a larger lesson in the Latin letters, especially now as I type them on the page: A.M.D.G. I think that, as T.S. Eliot wrote, we stand on the shoulders of those who have gone before us. Those whose words, whose intellects, whose spirits are the gifts we inherit. From them we make a different world than theirs but we build our extension bridges always from the solid pylons they provided.

As a writer and a teacher I've had excellent models for language: John Henry Newman, T.S. Eliot, Dylan Thomas, William Stafford, and Annie Dillard—to name a few—who taught me the textures of words, the delicacy of diction, the intricacy of sentence weaving. Those are good things to have, as is the simple joy in language which makes teaching such a pleasure.

But language is, as Hamlet said, "Words, words, words..." And, without the embodiment of soul and of purpose, no matter how beautifully words are strung together, they are as lifeless as the mannequins in a department store window. Each writer who has had the pleasure of ultimately seeing a work published, a poem, a story, an essay which moved someone else, knows that when words come alive it is a combination of craft and inspiration that is fortuitous and often quite beyond the writer's modest talents. It has to do with powers outside the author; it has to do with spirit.

For me the gift of spirit came from my grandmother, a woman everyone called Mame when I was a child. She was a Mame or Madame in the Old World sense: buxom, wholesome, with a Victorian propriety which had survived three wars (the Spanish-American, the Great War, and the Second) and a lost son, my uncle, in the last.

She knew more than most parents and most Jesuits about values like courage, generosity and smiling stoicism, and could quote chapter and verse if needed. She honored me with a spontaneous, uncritical love which expressed itself in hearty breakfasts of bacon, doughboys (delicious medallions of quickbread), buttered scrambled eggs and coffee sweetened with cream from the top of the bottle. She favored me and pampered me as one does with the last of the male line.

One day, as I was coming home from my fifth grade class, some older boys took my tweed Irish cap from off my head and tossed it around like a football. When I tried to get it back, they teased me into tears and then contemptuously threw the hat up into the branches of a maple tree.

I ran to Mame's house, dried my tears, and then sat down waiting for the vanilla wafers and iced ginger ale which was an afternoon ritual. None appeared. Instead of greeting me with her usual warmth, she was sitting quietly by a window seat from which she had obviously witnessed my humiliation.

"Where are the cookies, Grandma?" I asked.

She looked up with no hint of a twinkle in her blue eyes.

"Where is your tweed cap?" she asked.

"Some boys took it," I said. "Big boys," I added so she would not think me too much of a coward.

"Then, you'll have to get it back," she answered. And there was a hardness in her voice that I had never guessed possible.

"Will you go with me, Grandma?" I asked plaintively.

"No," she said. "That is one thing a grandma can't do for a boy. You must get it yourself, and you must do it for me because I can't afford to buy you another."

"But what will I say to them?" I whined.

She turned to me with a fierce Irish face and, with a voice I could never have imagined, spat out: "You get that damn cap out of the tree, now!"

I went back to the school yard and, without a second's hesitation, went up to the biggest of the boys: "You get that damn cap out of the tree, now!" The boy, too shocked by my bold tone or too cowardly, climbed up the tree branch and tossed down the cap. The others looked idly on. I marched back to Mame's house, my pride at accomplishment tinged slightly with wonder, and sat down to my usual treat of vanilla wafers and ginger ale. Nothing more was ever said, and the incident was never repeated.

The words she gave me, the inflection, the tough snarl that I imitated, worked. They empowered me in a way which seemed magical then. But I understand now that the spiritual force behind those words was love, and the fear of loss that the tweed cap represented. Something given in love, I learned, is irreplaceable and thus must be fiercely cherished.

When Mame died I was the altar boy at the high mass and followed the priest around her bronze-handled coffin with the thurible in a cloud of incense intoning the words of the *Dies Irae* in Latin: "The day of wrath when the heavens and the earth shall be moved and the

Lord will come to judge…" The tears streamed down my face, and I was inconsolable. My grandfather was even more so. He died himself three months later from a heart which, though previously sound, suddenly stopped as if broken.

Each time I sit down to write, each time I walk into a classroom, Mame is with me. The uncritical love in her eyes, the clear inflection, the willingness to make unequivocal challenges to the child she loved. Thinking of her I know that all of our gifts, whether they be Irish caps, or language, or a student's grasp of a new idea, are blessed by love and irreplaceable. They are to be cherished, and are always worth speaking up for, fiercely when necessary. And not out of arrogance or pride, but "*ad majorem Dei gloriam,*" this one life, these school days, and words spoken from the heart.

ON CANYONS AND CANCER CELLS

It is hard to explain to youngsters the intensity of our grief when John Kennedy was assassinated in 1963. How the tears came as we sat watching the funeral cortege pass and the riderless horse prance down Pennsylvania Avenue. Those tears were a measure of who we were as a people, our deep understanding of the magnitude of our loss. Few of us cried when we heard the news of the Valdez oil spill, or when we saw the results in the newspaper photographs and t.v. clips. The outrage was there, the violation of our sensibilities. But no tears for the greatest environmental murder of our generation, for the birds dying by the thousands soaked in tar, the ecological balance permanently altered.

If Ed Abbey were alive he would have cried. He was that kind of man. He loved the earth that much, was so connected to it that he felt each stupid, painful waste of its beauty and resources as a personal loss.

Ed Abbey died last year at the age of sixty-two.[1] He was an environmental activist and a naturalist as well as one of the finest prose writers of our generation. His books celebrated the natural beauty of America while bemoaning its imminent destruction. For most of us and our children the only place left to experience Ed Abbey's America is in his books. Many of the pristine canyons he hiked have been de-

---

1. A shorter version of this essay was first published in 1989 in the *Albany Review*; Abbey had died the year before.

stroyed by the construction of dams; many of the once-virginal forests
he roamed have been clear-cut by the lumber industry.

Abbey warned us that greed, personal and corporate, was throwing
our lives out of balance. He felt that this was not just apparent where
corporate profit in oil and lumber was more important that wildlife,
ecological balance and open space. It was apparent, too, in cities where
decent housing and a compassionate way of life were subordinated to
unlimited growth and real estate speculation.

In 1986 Abbey was official writer-in-residence for the City of San
Francisco, on assignment for the *Examiner*. He had a thoughtful reply
to then-mayor Diane Feinstein's dictum that "a city not growing is a
city dying." Abbey suggested: "Why not consider that a city, like a man
or a woman or a tree or any healthy living thing, should grow until it
reaches maturity—and then stop. Life begins at maturity. Think of it
this way, Mayor Feinstein: When a city stops growing its citizens can
finally begin to live. In peace. Security."

Abbey saw only two possible solutions to the continuous spiral of
growth. Either we reduce our standard of living to something like the
Asian level, or we restrict further population growth and immigration.
His proposals to do the latter were decried as eugenics and as racism.
But as the *No Vacancy* signs proliferate across America this summer we
would do well to begin considering the fact that our boat is full and in
peril of sinking. We cannot adequately care for the people who wander
homeless in our streets. We cannot take care of the children abandoned,
born addicted. One local social service agency recently had a "show-
case" of 150 such children to try to interest prospective foster parents.
Shades of the auction block, or even sadder, of the Christmas display in
Gump's Department Store of the abandoned pets who had, one might
add, a much better chance at adoption.

Something must be done, it is obvious. We are gradually becoming
a nation of people we cannot respect. Homeless beggars stand outside

the barricaded and bullet-proofed concert halls as bejeweled and gowned ladies are escorted by polished gentlemen to the Black and White Ball in San Francisco. Echoes of 1789 and Marie Antoinette's "Let them eat cake!" A reflection of the disparity of class which we generally associate with undeveloped nations, or historically imperiled ones.

We are no longer morally obliged, Abbey wrote, to be a "safety valve" for the teeming millions of the Third World. We cannot continue to take the troubled overflow of populations which double every thirty years. We are in danger of becoming a macrocosm of the nations they're evacuating or something even worse. Ideology and nationalistic pride in our "open door" policy are not enough.

What about the rest of us? Those who are neither begging for change in the street nor dancing in the chandeliered ballroom. You know, the people who go to work every day, save their money, and have through grace or luck avoided crushing economic failure or catastrophic illness. Those of us who have progressed to the point where we're no longer living from paycheck to paycheck but still have, as Abbey writes, "no homes to call our own but a few cells in the urban hive." And increasingly little chance to buy one. What about us?

Some of the solutions Abbey proposed a few years ago appear less and less outrageous as we become increasingly overwhelmed by the alternative. One of his proposals was a moratorium on immigration. Another was to revise the tax system so as to reward singles and childless couples, thus requiring the begetters of children to pay more, not less, in taxes. Another was to offer economic incentives to welfare mothers who do *not* produce, instead of the other way around. Hard and unpopular solutions which were rejected out of hand by those who had no others to offer.

Ed Abbey lived a life of order, frugality, and passion, spending a good deal of time with the beauty of the natural world. He also lived a life of creativity and service to his fellow man. He wrote to tell us how the possibility of that kind of life was fading and that, if we didn't make some hard decisions, the good life would be unavailable to future generations. He told us that we were trading our heritage for trinkets: the rich forests and open range, wild rivers and breathtaking canyons, lush meadows and rolling hills, for "bright slick robot-manufactured junk, none of which, not a single item of which, we actually need." He wrote that "unlimited growth is the etiology of the cancer cell." It was his surest and most prophetic metaphor.

And, as for the cities, we already know that, despite the overpriced concerts and balls, they are not the centers of civilization we'd like them to be. Both those who arrive at the balls in their tuxedoes and gowns and the hungry beggars outside are equally demeaned. And those who do not feel so have already experienced that hardening of sensitivity which is the antithesis of real culture.

In this "regressive, greedy and servile decade," Abbey wrote in 1986, "Americans are gradually becoming the kind of people we have historically despised." These were hard words from a harsh critic, but they were from a man who loved his country and its (*not* limitless) possibilities. Abbey decried the abdication by other writers of their important role of speaking of these things. He believed in presenting the unpopular truths about our country in the hope of preserving it, and of owing allegiance—not to government or majority opinion—but to truth. He believed like Samuel Johnson that "a writer's duty was to make the world better."

The works of some writers should be re-read at critical points in our civilization to remind us of who we are and what we are becoming. Ed Abbey's books are in that category. He reminded us that growth is not the ultimate purpose of a civilization. Unlimited growth *is* "the etiology of the cancer cell." And, as Abbey ominously added, while "cancer has no purpose but growth; it does have another result—the death of the host." —*San Francisco, 1989*

When I first wrote this article for the *Albany Review* over a decade ago, I had not lived south of the border. My only experiences with Mexico were fleeting ones in the border towns of Nogales or Tijuana. Since then I have lived eleven years in Central Mexico and travelled widely throughout Latin America. I still admire the voice of Ed Abbey, his unforgettable metaphor on the etiology of the cancer cell, and his willingness to speak up for strong measures. My thoughts on immigration and the United States "having no moral obligation to the Third World," however, have changed.

Flying over Mexico City last month through mile after mile of brown air so thick one could barely make out the buildings below, or the hundreds of thousands of cars, the factories, the mills and processing plants, I observed the results of "urban development" more closely, as Mexico rushes to join the First World economy. It is a Dickensian London, or a Pittsburgh of the 1890s, tacked on to a culturally rich and diversely beautiful city. What has saved it so far from revolution or, even worse, brutal anarchy, is the deep spirituality of the people, the integrity of the family, and the strength of its social institutions and its culture. But all of these have reached the breaking point.

In the streets below me were more than 20 million people. More than Tokyo, more than Beijing. It is the largest city in the world. Some of those people were immigrants from Guatemala, El Salvador, Nicaragua—refugees, homeless women and children, victims of policies dictated or supported by our State Department. So, I ask myself, is it Mexico's moral obligation to take care of hundreds of thousands of Central Americans forced from their homes at gunpoint by repressive regimes, by Contra soldiers, by death squads, most (if not all) tacitly supported by U.S. funds and U.S. troops? Why should Mexico inherit the whirlwind of U.S. policies in Central America?

As I travel around the country, I see foreign businessmen in Monterrey, Puebla and Guadalajara encouraging growth industries with the same missionary zeal that Mormons proselytize their faith. Japanese, Americans, West Germans, all competing for this developing market. I see the environmental stresses caused by burgeoning industry: denuded forests, polluted rivers, bitter-choking air, dengue fever, amoebic dysentery, tuberculosis, mental retardation from the high lead content in the air. I see the villages empty out as more and more young people go to the cities for jobs that don't exist without a level of training which they have not got and have no chance of getting. I see the stresses build up in the cities, cities just south of our border where we cannot afford to see a major revolution or anarchistic terror. Now, more and more, the pressure valve of immigration seems to make sense. Not only as a moral obligation, but as a practical way of dealing with the seeds we have sown. Besides, the areas to which these marginal Mexicans "emigrate" are lands which before the U.S. War of Intervention (1846-48) were theirs: California, Arizona, New Mexico. There seems a poetic justice in that.

Yet, immigration aside, I know, as Robert Kaplan observed in *The Coming Anarchy*, that the environmental issue truly "is the national security issue of the 21st century." I also know now that it is not merely the environment of the United States, as Ed Abbey suggested, which is the issue. It is, after all, a small planet. What happens in Latin America affects us. International corporations, policies of the World Trade Organization, decisions of the international banking community, all have an impact on water depletion, air pollution, deforestation, soil erosion, and the spread of disease. What we do in our neighbor's backyard will sooner or later affect our own. And from what I've seen in the past decade, it will be sooner rather than later.

As I watched the news on t.v. this past year and saw the marchers in Seattle outside the World Trade Organization meetings, and then later in Washington, D.C., protesting the I.M.F. policies, it occurred to me that only one thing was wrong with the picture. It was the fact that there was no one *inside* those meetings presenting the issues of the protesters. Left and right, conservative and liberal, democratic and authoritarian, are no longer viable dichotomies in the real world of the 21st century. As the techno-optimists at the World Trade Organization are celebrating the advances of unbridled capitalism and telling us how human ingenuity will solve whatever problems materialize, Mexico City staggers along, trying to remedy the (perhaps irreversible) damage already done to the ecosystem, to manage an underclass that cannot afford the basic U.N. caloric daily intake, to quell unrest among its students whose rising expectations have been ill-served by an indecisive government compromised by privatization and corporate ambition. The solutions to Mexico City's problems—ingenious ones being developed by engineers, social planners, economists and agronomists—may already be too late.

The United States, West Germany, Japan, the W.T.O., the I.M.F., and international corporations have all played a part in creating this crisis. We cannot sit idly by and hope that Catholic Charities and other N.G.O.'s will pick up the slack. While Border Patrol agents stand guard over illegals at the Nogales checkpoint, airborne diseases (caused by deforestation) never seen before in the United States pass easily through customs; rumblings are heard of revolution in the hills of Guerrero, in the jungles of Chiapas; cities are becoming unlivable, dangerous and crime infested, with air so polluted that school children in Mexico City are not allowed to play ball outside in the winter; and the agricultural fields and villages which sustained the nation's poor for centuries have been abandoned by the young people needed most desperately to work in them.

If the U.S. wants to retain any moral superiority in the 21st century, it must insist that the issues of the Seattle protesters be part of corporate planning, of W.T.O. decision making, and of international business policy. I am not so naive as to assume that even a superpower can accomplish the radical transformation of international agencies, transnational corporations, or other nations' developmental policies. But it can assume leadership, a leadership more in tune with lasting values and the long-term interests of its citizens than with the illusion of progress generated by the out-of-control growth which threatens to destroy its host. It might begin by having the I.M.F. and the World Bank open their books and correct policies which have deepened poverty in Latin American nations while ensuring a constant flow of interest to wealthy countries. It might answer Pope John Paul II's challenge to lender nations to forgive the debts of poorer ones in the light of the dawn of the third millennium. It might respond to the unanswered second challenge of John F. Kennedy's inaugural: "Ask what together we can do for the freedom of mankind."

THE DAY A REINDEER LOST HIS HEAD

The Monday before Christmas we high school teachers at the American School of Guadalajara were called together for a staff meeting. We were reminded of the high absence rate the day before Thanksgiving break. We were told that this was because teachers had developed a cavalier attitude toward teaching the day before holidays and that as a result, students did not take coming to school seriously on those days. Neither did their parents.

Most of the teachers thought that making the day before the holiday a *half*-day, with twenty minutes periods (including recess) and dismissal at noon, might have a good deal more to do with it. However, we held our collective tongues.

"The day before *Christmas* break, however, is going to be different," announced our vice-principal, Mr. Herrera.

"A *full* school day then?" one teacher asked.

"No. No, still a half-day. But just to make sure all the students are taking it seriously, I'm going to ask each and every one of you to give a quiz. Anyone who is absent that day will receive a zero. This will insure that there will be *serious* teaching going on and that the students will be occupied during the full twenty minute period."

I had just finished reading and correcting 128 book reports two days earlier. A prodigious task. I had a clearly defined lesson plan for the remainder of the week with clearly articulated goals. I did not feel disposed to grading 128 English quizzes simply for the purpose of keeping my students occupied. I said so.

"Well," Mr. Herrera replied, "I am going to check the classes to make sure there is relevant teaching going on."

"That's fine," I said.

"*Meaningful* teaching, Mr. Hogan," he added.

"I understand," I said.

Each year I read a Christmas piece from Dickens or O. Henry or Dylan Thomas (depending on the class level) and pass out song sheets of English Christmas carols. After the reading we sing along. Since it is an English class and the students are learning both English pronunciation and tradition in this period, I consider it highly appropriate. I was a bit concerned, however, with Mr. Herrera's warning. There was a possibility he might not agree with me, and that my traditional Christmas class offering might be considered frivolous. Also, it was possible that some of the parents, convinced that no real teaching was going on during this half-day session, would not encourage their children to attend. Or, that the kids themselves (some of whom had me for English last year) would not bother to come. I was already preparing my defense.

The Friday before Christmas arrived cool and clear. Students were bringing gaudily-wrapped presents for friends and teachers. There was evidence of candies, cookies and other treats that the students would share at recess. The mood was festive. In my first four classes there were only five absences out of ninety-six students. Something of a record.

In the ninth grade class I read O'Henry's "The Gift of the Magi." It is the story, you might remember, of a poor couple who are more or less broke as the holidays approach. The wife has only $1.98 in savings. But she has beautiful hair: gorgeous tresses which flow down past her waist. Her hair is her most valuable possession. Notwithstanding this fact, she goes to a hair broker, has her hair cut off and obtains twenty dollars. With this money she is able to but a watch chain for her husband. She knows this will be an ideal Christmas present because he has a beautiful silver watch which he loves to show off. However, it is currently fastened to his waistcoat with a poor leather strap.

When he arrives home he is somewhat nonplussed to see his wife's beautiful hair has been cut off. Still, he loves her and still finds her beautiful. She explains what happened to the hair: "I sold it to buy this lovely chain for your watch." Unfortunately, however, the husband had pawned the watch to buy the wife a beautiful comb for her (once glorious and highly treasured) hair. The story ends with a reference to the Magi which I thought significant and wanted to talk about. I wanted to say how when we truly love someone we want to give them the most valuable thing we possess.

However, I got no further than the part about the comb when my voice quavered and tears came to my eyes. The poignancy and beauty of the story overwhelmed me. Alejandra, a sensitive ninth grader, volunteered to complete the reading for me. The class was quiet and thoughtful when she finished; moved, as I hoped they would be, by this tender and simple tale about the true meaning of Christmas. I felt that no matter what the rest of the day held, it was already a success.

Then came recess. It was relatively quiet; kids exchanging presents, having snacks, until suddenly from the primary side of the school there appeared like a vision (a noisy one at that) Santa Claus and his eight shiny reindeer. The pasteboard reindeer were quite lifelike and behind them was a human Santa in a great sleigh. The whole contraption was mounted on a large 7-UP soft drink truck. "Jingle Bells" was playing from a loud speaker and the serious tone of the secondary school was shattered.

The high school students were given a few moments of grace to watch the spectacle of Santa circling the athletic field and then they were to return to their classes. Unfortunately, the reindeer and the sleigh were a bit higher off the ground than the driver had anticipated and, as he passed close to the trees, CRASH! The starboard lead reindeer's horns got caught in the branches. "*¡CUIDATE, CABRÓN!*" yelled Santa.

CRACK! And, as the sleigh moved on, off came the head of Dancer (or Prancer), as Rudolph went merrily forward.

"*¡A LA CHINGADA CON TODO!*" screamed Santa. "*¿NO ME OYES, CABRÓN?*"

"*¿*WHO ARE YOU CALLING '*CABRÓN*', *CABRÓN*? yelled the driver.

Meanwhile Mr. Herrera arrived at the scene along with Miss Soledad Avalos, the Principal. "Please, please," they begged. "No swearing, please! The children. This is Christmas time."

"Tell that to this *cabrón* of a Santa," said the driver of the 7-UP truck. "We only hired him because his sister-in-law is a friend of the owner."

"They only hired *you* because you married the accountant's cousin," countered Santa. "You don't even have a driver's license, cabrón."

"Please, please!" implored the Vice-Principal. "The children, please! What kind of Santa Claus are you anyway?"

Meanwhile all the kids have gathered around, making good-natured gibes.

"The truck driver doesn't have a license. Hey, Santa, do *you* have a license?" asked Julio.

"Some Santa Claus. He swears like a fire eater," remarked Gonzalo.

"Maybe he's a retired fire eater," suggested Julio.

"The truck driver's nose is redder than Rudolph's," Pati laughed.

"Hey, Mr. Hogan," said Fernando. "Write a poem about the reindeer losing his head."

"Yeah, Mr. Hogan," another student added. "Write a poem that we can *understand* for a change."

By now the bell had rung for the students to return to classes.

"All right, all right," I said. "That's enough. Let's get going."

"How about the poem, Mr. Hogan?" Fernando persisted. "Come on, a Christmas present for us."

"Okay," I said. "You've got my word. I'll write a poem about it. Now, [I assumed my most serious demeanor] let's get to English class. The bell has already rung."

When everybody was finally settled down in my tenth grade class I read them Dylan Thomas' "A Child's Christmas in Wales." When I was finished and pretty nearly out of breath from Thomas' pyrotechnics, I passed out the song sheets. We sang "Silent Night," "O Come All Ye Faithful," and "Angels We Have Heard On High." Vicki and Ana Karina in the back of the room were not singing but…

We had just reached "GLO—OOOOO—OOOOO—OOOOO—REE—AH IN EXCELSIS DEO" when the Vice-Principal came in the door. He looked around the class, smiled, and then picked up a song sheet. He joined us for the next stanza and a chorus, singing with gusto in a surprisingly good voice.

"Beautiful, Mike," he said. "Really fine."

"Yeah," I said, figuring I knew what he meant and remembering Alejandra in the ninth grade finishing the O. Henry story, and the understanding silence of the students. Knowing that their instincts were usually good, given a chance.

"Yeah," I said again. "They are beautiful, aren't they?"

"By the way," he asked. "Did you hear the language of that Santa?"

"How could I help it," I said. "Fernando thinks I should write a poem about Dancer losing his head."

"Who?" he asked.

"The reindeer, you know," I said.

"A reindeer named Fernando?" he asked.

"Never mind," I said, turning back to my class.

And now everybody was singing, even Vicki and Ana Karina, even macho Jimmy and Hector, and their voices rose in the clear December

air: GLOR—OOOOO—OOOOO—OOOOO—REE—AH IN
EXCELSIS DE—EE—OO.

I pride myself on knowing when to end an essay. But I also try to
keep my promises. So, at the risk of ruining a perfectly good narrative
with a scrap of meritless doggerel, I nevertheless append the following
"poem" in fulfillment of my promise to Fernando.

CHRISTMAS POEM FOR FERNANDO

"We've got to be serious," Herrera said,
And laid down his rules Procrustean.
I disagreed and held instead
That at Christmas time we must be in

A different mood than tests and marks,
A mood of song, of sharing, giving;
Not materialism or childish larks
But the *sine qua non* of living.

Then Santa came with a driver *crudo*,
His eyes bloodshot, shouting inanely.
The sleigh was driven in such a way, Oh!
Beneath the trees he swerved insanely.

Off came the horns and then the head
Of Dancer, the reindeer, the starboard lead.
Then Santa swore as poor Dancer bled,
And one girl laughed so hard she peed.

Herrera was more annoyed than ever.
"A SERIOUS day I had planned," he said.
Now it will be remembered forever
As the day the reindeer lost his head.

CONNECTIONS:
ODYSSEUS AND THE GRAN CHINGÓN

Searching for the origins of a particular cultural trait is more often facilitated by history or sociology than by literature. Thus we might trace Americans' work ethic to the early Pilgrims, or Japanese formality to a homogenous society. Yet, the origin of the Latin quality of *machismo* has its roots in ancient Greek literature, a pervasive work composed by Homer four centuries before writing was even invented. *Machismo* is a durable trait and has survived well into the 20th century in Latin America despite inroads by modern society, feminism, and generalized middle class values. How a character trait from ancient Greece came to be adopted by countries then undiscovered and far distant in both geography and culture, is a tale worth telling.

Just recently a Mexican bank, promoting the benefits of its credit cards, sponsored a t.v. commercial which showed an elegant young man named Gastón Gastalón who is presented the restaurant bill for a large table of his friends and associates. The men all confidently reach the check, each one offering to pay, but Gastón Gastalón prevails. "*Yo invito, yo pag*o," he confidently announces. But when he checks his wallet, he finds that he has insufficient funds to cover the bill. The waiter looks at him with contempt, and the other diners turn away in embarrassment at his public humiliation. The announcer then cuts in: "If you wish to be a Gastón Gastilón, always carry your Banamex card."

Gastón Gastalón is obvious rhyming slang for the *Gran Chingón*, a type briefly characterized by Octavio Paz in *The Labyrinth of Solitude*, his seminal work on the Mexican character. The *gran chingón* typifies the essence of the macho character. Some of his more obvious qualities are unshakable self-confidence, a paternalistic attitude toward family and employees, and an unwillingness to take advice from others. He tends to be xenophobic and distrusts foreigners. He is both outspoken and demonstrative about his love of his wife, yet he often has a mistress and flirts with other women. In business or in politics he will not only try to defeat his competition but will go out of his way to humiliate and demean them. From this latter trait he got his name. *Chingón* is derived from the verb *chingar* which means to rape, or to screw. A *chingazo* is a screwup; *no me chingues* means don't screw with me. Notes Octavio Paz:

> The verb chingar *signifies the triumph of the closed, the male, the powerful, over the open. If we take into account all of its various meanings, the word defines a great part of our life and qualifies our relationships with our friends and compatriots. To the Mexican there are only two possibilities in life: either he inflicts the actions implied by* chingar *on others, or else he suffers them himself at the hands of others. This conception of social life as combat fatally divides society into the strong and the weak. The strong—the hard, unscrupulous* chingones—*surround themselves with eager followers. This servility toward the strong, especially among the* políticos *(that is, the professionals of public business), is one of the most deplorable consequences of the situation.... The verb* chingar—*malign and agile and playful, like a caged animal—creates many expressions that turn our world into a jungle: there are tigers in business, eagles in the schools, and the army, lions among our friends.*

The *gran chingón* does not show his emotions nor does he ever let anyone get the better of him. He drinks but he never gets drunk, never loses control. He is courageous and strong. However, he often detracts from these positive qualities by being a *presumido* or braggart with respect to his accomplishments.

These elements of character do not describe one man, but rather a type of man who will be immediately recognized in business, politics, the military, the academy by his contemporaries. He is the *macho* character. In addition to the qualities mentioned above, he is often good looking, charismatic, and charming which combine to make the sum of these characteristics seem less stereotypical, and more a fairly well-rounded description of a man of some importance in Latin society. Anyone who has lived in Latin America has met the *gran chingón* in one guise or another: a boss, a political figure, a father, a brother, a husband. How did this personality develop? Why is it so endemic especially in Latin countries? Why is it, despite criticism especially from the affluent and well-educated middle class, still persistent? Why, despite the criticism, is it also secretly admired not only by men but also by women? What are the origins of the *gran chingón*?

The answers to these questions seem to be in *The Odyssey*, that pervasive epic which has been taught to schoolboys from the time education was first formalized. Socrates discussed it with Plato, Aristotle with Alexander, and masters throughout the Middle Ages taught it to their pupils at the University of Paris, the University of Toledo, and at the medieval church schools in Rome, in Barcelona and Madrid. Keep in mind that girls were not taught in any of these schools. Education was a male prerogative. Classics, especially the Greek classics, were presented not only to teach language skills, history and statecraft, but also to mold the character of these young men. They were to be the next leaders of their societies, either secular or religious. What models presented themselves for their study in the Greek classics? The most accessible certainly was Odysseus. He also had the distinct advantage of having been "Christianized" to some extent by the monks' translations of the original Greek. Odysseus was the first "hero" of classic education whom the young man could emulate, and upon whose character he could model his own. Odysseus was courageous, he was able to think three steps ahead, he was crafty, self-reliant, but also believed in a deity which gave him strength which doubled his own. Odysseus was willing to leave his homeland in search of honor and wealth, a quality much to be encouraged as the European empires looked westward to conquest. By the 16th century, the heroic qualities of Odysseus could be observed in Vasco de Gama, Magellan, Balboa, Columbus and Cortéz as they set forth on their own odysseys in the New World. This pantheon of heroes would be models for coming generations of youngsters in the Americas, both the educated ones who read their Homer and saw the connections, and those less educated who saw only the local model or *cacique*.

I use the word "hero," even though these men were flawed, some tragically, because it is this flawed heroic model which provides the root of *machismo*. The flaws are intrinsic to the character of the first model: Odysseus himself.

Even today Odysseus is presented as a hero in all the textbooks taught to school children. Commonly covered in the ninth grade literature curriculum, as well as world history texts in both middle school and high school, the heroic qualities of Odysseus are undisputed by scholastic editors. Not only was he brave facing monsters such as the Cyclops, Scylla and Charybdis, but he was also extremely clever in *The Iliad* outwitting the Trojans with the famous wooden horse. He was resourceful, ingenious, coolheaded in combat, and indefatigable. He never gave up even when the odds were against him, even when he apparently had lost everything. His heroic qualities, however, are so inextricably bound up with his *gran chingón* qualities that it seems unlikely the average teacher could have time or patience to unravel them. That being so, it is no wonder that boys find that in accepting Odysseus as a hero, they uncritically accept as well the aspects of his personality which have more to do with the *gran chingón* than with the traditional hero whom the teacher would like the child to emulate.

In the first book of *The Odyssey* we are introduced to the central character who tells us in a few words just who he is. "I am Laertes' son, Odysseus. Men hold me formidable for guile in peace and war: this fame has gone abroad to the sky's rim." He is both proud of his heritage and a bit arrogant. He brags about his ability to use guile, that is, to deceive people. However, while this may be a good quality for a leader in wartime, one hesitates to find it attractive for a peacetime leader. Most agree it is a good idea to fool the enemy (the wooden horse, for example), but few citizens find deception an attractive quality in a leader within the peaceful confines of his own nation (Richard Nixon's fate seems to be sufficient proof of this).

Although he loves his wife, Odysseus has been seduced by Calypso, "loveliest of goddesses," and by "Circe, the enchantress" who "detained me... but in my heart, I never gave consent." Like the *gran chingón,* he loves his wife, the mother of his children, but he makes love quite passionately and uninhibitedly with paramours, although the other women never mean anything really, since he does not formally "give consent" to them. The concept of fidelity for the *gran chingón* can perversely include infidelity, and is justifiable as long as he makes no commitment, gives no consent or legitimacy, to the extramarital relationship. I am reminded of *The Bridges of Madison County* in this regard, another book in which the bonds of matrimony seems similarly flexible, only in that book (and film) from a female standpoint. The absence of inhibition, or of remorse, on the part of the female protagonist, however, is similar to that of Odysseus. Perhaps a by-product of the subliminal influence of such texts, now that classes are no longer limited to young males as they were in the Middle Ages.

When he comes to the Island of the Cyclopes we see how astute Odysseus is. Noticing the unharvested grapes on the island he assumes quite rightly that the Cyclopes have not yet developed the skills to ferment wine. This being the case, they certainly have not learned the more complex science of distilling brandy. He thus formulates a plan to get the Cyclops drunk on a powerful brandy he has brought with him.

He raids his cave, steals cheeses and other comestibles, and when Odysseus' men suggest that they leave before the giant comes back Odysseus refuses. The Cyclops, a foreigner, is demeaned by Odysseus as less than human ("a brute so huge, he seemed no man at all") which reveals the *gran chingón* characteristic of xenophobia. Yet, Odysseus is willing to put the lives of his men in jeopardy, in order to observe this stranger at close hand, dominate him if he can, use his guile upon him, and humiliate him.

When the Cyclops returns, he does, in fact, take umbrage at the breaking and entering of his home by Odysseus and his men. He proceeds to devour several of Odysseus' crew. Odysseus gives him some brandy to drink, waits until he passes out, and then carries out his plan to "chingar" him, or quite literally screw him. He cuts out a six foot section of a wooden beam and hews it to make a stake with a pointed end. He holds it in the fire until the tip is red hot. Then he rams the pole deep into the eye of the Cyclops. This act, which is the occasion of one of the most powerful of Homer's extended similes, is an ugly and gratuitous rape of the Cyclops:

> So with our brand we bored that great eye socket
> while blood ran out around the red-hot bar.
> Eyelid and lash were seared; the pieced ball
> hissed broiling, and the roots popped.
>   In a smithy
> one sees the white-hot axhead or an adz
> plunged and wrung in a coldtub, screeching steam—
> the way they make soft iron hale and hard:
> just so that eyeball hissed around the spike.

The enthusiasm with which this scene is described is significant. The Greek poet does not turn away from this gratuitous violence, he revels in it. This is how a hero deals with his enemies, never mind that the Cyclops has done him no wrong. He is "other," a foreigner, less than human. Earlier, when the Cyclops asked Odysseus his name, Odysseus told him, "Nobody." Now as the Cyclops screams out in the night, his fellow Cyclopes respond: "Who has tricked you? Who has ruined you?" The Cyclops replies; "Nobody's tricked me. Nobody's ruined me." And that, of course, obviates any chance of help from his countrymen since "nobody has played you foul in your lonely bed." Notice the choice of words, however. "To ruin," "to play foul in bed," are both references to violation, to rape, which is literally what Odysseus has done.

Odysseus manages to escape from the cave after the blinding of the Cyclops and passes right under his face, hidden beneath the rams whom the Cyclops lets out in the morning to pasture. Once out of the cave, however, instead of making good his escape from the island, Odysseus stands in his boat a few meters off shore and taunts the Cyclops. Bragging about what he has done, he tells the Cyclops his name. The Cyclops throws a boulder at his ship, almost sinking it, and Odysseus' men ask Odysseus to please desist and get the ships safely out to sea. But Odysseus, in his *presumido* element, ignores them:

> I would not heed them in my glorying spirit,
> but let my anger flare and yelled:
>   "Cyclops,
> if ever moral man inquire
> how you were put to shame and blinded, tell him
> 'Odysseus, raider of cities, took your eye:
> Laertes' son, whose home is Ithaca!' "

A good leader usually sacrifices his own ego to protect his crew, Odysseus does the opposite. In fact, throughout *The Odyssey* we see Odysseus put his men's lives in jeopardy, lose crew after crew, until it has become a refrain, "Our precious lives we had but not our friends," and he ends up alone clinging to a mast *sans* crew, *sans* ships, *sans* friends.

When his men get intoxicated on the island of Lotus eating the hallucinatory leaves of the lotus plant, Odysseus wisely refrains. The *gran chingón* does not use drugs, or anything else which might allow him to lose control. Control is essential to him as is clear-mindedness. Those who eat of the lotus, like modern day pot heads, "never cared to report, nor to return: they longed to stay forever browsing on that native bloom, forgetful of their homeland." So, he drives them back to the ship and throws them in chains. He has zero tolerance for drugs, as do most Latin American leaders. The war on drugs seems to them very much a Yankee problem, the self-indulgence of a country whose surplus wealth and lack of restraint makes it the largest consumer of drugs in the world. The paternalistic Latin has his children much more restrained, more controlled, more in tune with the values of the family.

On the other hand, Odysseus is so paternalistic that he does not give his men a chance to help him solve problems which occur; he does not listen to anyone's advice, and as a result jeopardizes both himself and his men on several occasions. The most notable of these is when they are faced with the decision to go through the straits guarded by Scylla and Charybdis. The former a six-headed monster, the latter a whirlpool. As he sends them toward Scylla he comments on his crew: "I told them nothing, as they could do nothing." It seems unlikely, however, that they could do nothing. Among his captains and navigators, all tested sailors who had been sailing for years, one at least might have been able to suggest an alternate route, or perhaps a pause in the journey until the whirlpool subsided (as it later did during a change in tide). Yet, Odysseus goes ahead anyway, and loses six of his best men.

Ultimately, as noted earlier, Odysseus loses all his ships and all his men. He is left alone on the ocean until he floats up on a log to the island of Calypso, "the dangerous nymph… who loved me…" where he stays until sated with sex and then, bored, he moves on. Finally, missing his home, and willing to accept help this time, even that of foreigners, Odysseus persuades the Phoenicians to provide him with a ship home.

Once back in Ithaca his guile returns. He disguises himself as a beggar so that he can spy on his wife Penelope and test her fidelity. A double standard here, since Odysseus was not only unfaithful but profligate in his infidelity. After assuring himself that she was indeed faithful, he turns to those who have abused his hospitality. Accompanied by his son Telemachus, he coldly proceeds to kill every one of the suitors who came to his house offering marriage to Penelope while he was gone. Despite the fact that only a handful actually violated his hospitality, and *they* offered to make amends in gold, Odysseus demands full payment in blood. He kills them all. This scene, reminiscent of the early Stephen King's novels for its microscopic descriptions of bloody carnage ends with this rich metaphor:

> Think of a catch that fishermen haul into a half-moon bay
> in a fine-meshed net from the whitecaps of the sea:
> how all are poured out on the sand, in throes for the salt sea,
> twitching their cold lives away in Helios' fiery air;
> so lay the suitors heaped on one another.

The story of the Odyssey is still popular with young people. It is exciting, violent, colorful, adventurous, and readily accessible. While its influence today in building the character of young men is certainly overshadowed by action films, biographies of rock stars, and exploits of athletes, the character formation which took place in Spain during the Middle Ages when it was the central work taught, cannot be so easily discounted. Moreover, since the friars and the conquistadors brought this educational background to Spanish America, and passed it on to their sons and male charges in mission schools and universities, its impact was relatively undiminished by its export to the New World.

Odysseus was taught as the model of what a leader should be. No wonder that so many Latin American leaders seem to be almost carbon copies: an eclectic mix of qualities which are often truly heroic such as valor, strong leadership, charisma, energy, intelligence and will to power; and others which are typically *gran chingón*, such as paternalism, xenophobia, braggadocio, arrogance, deceit, and violence (á la General Pinochet in Chile or the brutal days of the Díaz dictatorship in Mexico) against "perceived" enemies. As Octavio Paz wrote:

> *And in a world of chingones, of difficult relationships, ruled by violence and suspicion—a world in which no one opens out or surrenders himself—ideas and accomplishment count for little. The only thing of value is manliness, personal strength, a capacity for imposing oneself on others.*

Literature does have an effect on people, and whether it is simply absorbed to become part of the collective unconscious of a race, or whether it is examined, discussed and analyzed, can make a profound difference. The obligations of educators to more closely examine these works, to help their students to make connections, and to engage them in lively, analytical and critical thinking should be central to the job of teaching the next generation. Literature is about values and there is no pretending it's not. How those values are perceived and how they are inculcated is what the art of teaching is about.

ANILLO DE DIAMANTE

Thursday, July 11th. This is the day of the long-awaited eclipse and the skies at 10 a.m. are still overcast; there is a light drizzle. Nevertheless we are well-prepared and cautiously optimistic. I've borrowed two welder's helmets from the maintenance department at the school. The helmets have been cleaned and their protective visors smoothed with a chamois cloth. Lucinda has packed a picnic lunch of hard-boiled eggs, tunafish-stuffed bolillos, fresh tomatoes and, for dessert, chocolate brownies. There is a large umbrella in the trunk and a Platters' tape playing "Twilight Time" on the car stereo. We are headed to the *Bosque de Colomos*, a heavily wooded area on the outskirts of the city. My '78 Mercury Monarch (a.k.a. "Annie") is purring happily with a bellyful of Pemex gasoline, and we are in high spirits.

The eclipse, a 170-mile swath of darkness, will sweep the southern tip of Baja California, then speed down through Jalisco, Mexico City, Oaxaca and Chiapas, along the coast of Central America, and fade away in the basin of the Brazilian Amazon. The moon's shadow, travelling at almost twice the speed of sound, will take only 209 minutes to complete this incredible journey. The ETA of its appearance here in Guadalajara is 1:06 p.m.—Pacific Standard Time.

We have done quite a bit of reading and research on the eclipse. We want to be as fully informed as possible, not only because we are teachers, but because we want to participate fully in this phenomenon. Life is short and so much of it is lost in the trivial but necessary work of emptying the garbage, answering the mail, preparing classes, paying bills. So many moments of wonder are unattended, or attended to briefly. "We had the experience," as T.S. Eliot wrote, "but missed the meaning." Hopefully today we will be fully present. Not only informed, but awake, with all our senses alive and in tune.

This will be the longest total eclipse to pass over this part of the country since 1776, and its duration will not be surpassed until 2162. We've learned that detailed inspection of the corona (the halo which surrounds the sun and is visible only during a total eclipse) will reveal new information about the approximate age of the solar system and the creation of stars.

We know that in ancient China, eclipses were thought to occur when people had offended the gods. They believed that the gods then sent out a huge demon to eat the sun. People would rush out into the street with noisemakers, gongs, gunpowder and swords to try and frighten the dragon away. It invariably worked. The sun returned, either spit out or vomited up by the moon.

In India, eclipses were thought to be caused by people's sins. After people had sinned excessively the sun would begin to die. Hindus would rush by the thousands (later millions) to the sacred waters of the Ganges to cleanse themselves in the hope that the sun would shine again. This usually worked, too. But it did not contribute noticeably to the potability of the Ganges River water.

Europeans in the Middle Ages believed that an eclipse was an announcement of the coming of plagues, epidemics, war, or the end of the world. They believed these things despite the fact that a thousand years before, Arab astronomers knew about and were able to predict these phenomena, and had written numerous treatises on the subject. This is important to remember whenever we of European stock are tempted to feel superior to indigenous people who persist in strange beliefs.

Before the Spaniards arrived, the sun, personified by Huitzilopochtli, was the primary deity in Mexico. The influence of the sun god theology in Mexico has yet to be totally eliminated by Catholicism or by scientific argument. Many indigenous people still believe that the eclipse (imminent death of the sun god) can cause damaged crops and deformed children.

We've learned that there are an average of 66 eclipses each century, although most of these last only two or three minutes. All of the longer eclipses occur in June or July when the sun is furthest from the earth. We know that the maximum length of totality for a solar eclipse is seven minutes 40 seconds, and that the one today will last for six minutes and 14 seconds.

But there are a great many things we don't know. For example, what changes do the human eye perceive when looking at colors on the earth before, during, and after a total eclipse?

What happens to animals during a solar eclipse? Will a herd of cattle stampede? Will horses lie down, whinny nervously? Will they flash out with their hooves, gallop off in a panic?

Does the air become colder during an eclipse? Is there a wind? Do the birds assume it is night and fold their wings?

And, finally, how does the human observer feel? What emotions of dread or wonder, what primordial harkenings-back course through the blood? How does a crowd behave?

We hope to learn some of these things today.

We are already able to answer a few of the relatively simple questions the kids might ask. The most obvious one: How is it possible for the moon, which is so much smaller than the sun, to totally eclipse the sun with its shadow? The reason, of course, is that the moon's diameter happens to be equal proportionately to its distance from the sun. This in itself is extremely rare. The likelihood of this occurring anywhere else in the universe is infinitesimal. And here we have not only the phenomenon but also the intelligent life to witness it. That in itself places us under some obligation to be truly present this morning and to write down what we see and feel.

But while I am thinking this, I also recall that in *The Odyssey* (which I am teaching this year) the seer Theoclymenus predicts that on the day Odysseus will return and slay his wife's suitors, "the sun will perish out of heaven and an evil mist will spread over all." Undoubtedly an early reference to a solar eclipse. It is impossible to be pure observer when one is also a teacher. Always there is the search to find way to integrate relevant material into a lesson plan. *Basta*, content thee!

A young couple next to us in the parking lot leaves off their hugging to smile condescendingly as we unload our welder's masks from the trunk of the car and trudge up the rocky road toward the pasture where the horses are grazing. It is, after all, completely overcast and I'm sure they assume that, whatever phenomenon occurs this afternoon, there will not be sufficient sunlight to see more than the barest outlines. Besides, eye damage is the last thing on their minds. They only have eyes for each other. The eclipse and the six minutes of darkness will simply be an exponent for a lovers' walk in the woods. I stifle the brief feeling of being ridiculous, and smile back tolerantly.

I know that if the clouds relent at all, there will be sufficient danger in looking at the sun to fully justify our welder's outfits. Once the moon has come completely between the sun and the earth, the best way to see it is with the naked eye. However, before and after the total eclipse, looking at the sun is extremely dangerous without adequate protection. It can cause severe injury and even blindness. There have been several public service spots illustrating that on local t.v. One showed a scientist taking a lighted cigarette to the back of a cut-out plastic eyeball and burning it. "*Lo mismo*," he said. "This cigarette is doing the kind of damage you will do to your eyes if you look directly at the sun when it comes out of its total eclipse phase. And what is more, you won't feel any pain because the eye's retina is not sensitive to heat. You will not know you are injured until the damage is too late to reverse." That was enough for me. I'd rather look ridiculous than be blind. Besides the t.v. news also said that Honduran President Rafael Callejas has chosen this method to protect his eyes today. We are in good company. Chief Executive eyewear.

At noon the woods are noticeably darker. It feels like dusk. The partial phase commenced at 11:42. We go over to a field where the horses are grazing. There is a gray stallion with a white star on his forehead who gazes at us with a baleful eye. There is a dun-colored mare, and there is a colt on spindly legs close to her. The colt also has the white markings. Lucinda comments on the father's dominant genes.

We try to tempt the colt with an offer of an apple but he comes only halfway and then stops. He tries nibbling grass like his parents but his legs are so uncoordinated and so much longer than his neck that he stumbles awkwardly. Abandoning the effort, he bounds like a fawn over to the mother. There he finds a teat and begins to suck. The mare seems unaware of the approaching darkness. She gives suck and munches the rich grass with a self-possessed indifference.

There have been no major changes in the colors around us. The *lilas* are still clear blue. The leaves of the ivy are still waxy green and red. The bark of the trees unfaded, glistening from the morning's rain. Nothing really has changed except for the feel of approaching dusk. Some cars driving by have turned on their lights. Thunder rumbles in the distance and now and then a single drop of rain will hit my hand or bounce off my cap. But it could easily have been dropping from one of the cypress trees. The thunder is more threatening as it draws closer to 1 p.m.. It is a question now, which will occur first: a major deluge or the eclipse. The sky is still overcast and we are no longer quite sure of the exact position of the sun.

1:05 PM I head down the hill to get the umbrella out of the trunk of the car. The light has not changed nor has the cloud bank moved at all. The horses are contentedly cropping the grass. They have in fact moved from out of the partially-enclosed field and are grazing closer to where Lucinda has set up our camp on the hill. Some people are still riding around on the road that circles the wood, lights on, listening to the radio announcements concerning the eclipse (much like a football game play by play) but, annoyingly, not stopping their cars or getting out to feel it (even if they can't see it) for themselves.

1:09 PM By the time I have retrieved the umbrella and gotten back up the hill, the world is in total darkness. I felt, rather than saw, the shadows racing ahead of me as I ran. Despite my jacket and sweatshirt and the double-time hike up the hill, I am chilled. There has been a pronounced drop in temperature. (Later we will discover that it had fallen from 32 degrees to 26 degrees Centigrade in three minutes.) There was a noisy ratcheting of Sinaloan crows just prior to the darkness but now it is silent. I look for the horses but cannot see them. In fact, I can see very little because the lights on the roadway have come on, tripped by an electronic sensor. When I get off the road and into the woods I find Lucinda sitting on a log.

"Where are the horses?" I ask.

"I don't know," she says exasperated. "Why did you have to go for the stupid umbrella? I knew it would all happen as soon as you left."

We head up the hill for about two hundred yards. Not a sign of the horses. Not only the stallion and his family but the others have disappeared as well. And not a sound. Lucinda standing twenty feet away from the stallion did not hear his movement away from her on the soft earth. It was as if they had never been there—horses of our imagination.

It is totally dark now, and down below us we hear a wild cheer. There is an Art and Performance Center there and the students are sharing with the world their raucous delight at the phenomenon. Of course, anyone who has ever spent time around young people knows that lights going out during any public gathering is enough to get them shouting, stamping feet and whistling. But this sound is different. There it is again! Not that self-conscious and wiseguy sound of kids during a power outage, but a heartfelt cheer. The kind you seldom hear anymore, like when Audie Murphy took out the German tank in *To Hell and Back*, and the movie audience spontaneously applauded.

People don't cheer in movies anymore. They are too sophisticated. Actually, outside of sporting events (with half cheering for one side, half for the other) there isn't much cheering in the world. Most kids are too laid-back and most adults are too cynical. So this cheer of the teen-age kids below at the dancing school is unexpected, refreshing. Somewhere I remember hearing that joyful unabashed yell followed by applause before...

Then I remember. It was another July. Back in 1969. July 20th to be exact. When Neil Armstrong and Col. Edwin Aldrin scooped up the first lunar rocks and then bounced happily on the moon's low gravitational surface. The scene was beamed via satellite to a black and white t.v. at a bar in South Boston. A gang of longshoremen, neighborhood toughs, old salts, composed the audience. Talking, swearing, listening to country music on the jukebox. Suddenly the plug on the jukebox was pulled and everyone in the bar burst into applause. Not one hesitating; not one embarrassed. A more unlikely group you could not imagine, united for a time in the mystery of space. Part of the universe which extended far beyond the limits of South Boston (and the exigencies of their next drink, problems with the wife or the boss) had opened for them and suddenly they were ennobled.

The shouts and applause of the kids feel like that and a thrill rushes through me. And just then, the shadows fall away from the trees in a dizzying rush and the sun appears from behind a cloud. It could not be the full sun because the second phase will last at least until 2:38 p.m. and it is now only 1:15. Still, even this beginning spark of light has lit up the earth as if it were a bright summer morning. We hurriedly put on the welder's masks and there we see it! The *anillo de diamante*, pale gold circle around the sun with a large brilliant portion in the upper right corner like an enormous gem—the "diamond ring." Unquestionably the most exciting post-eclipse view of the sun.

We rest our eyes for a few seconds. Already the woods are bathed in what feels to be the fullness of the sun. We look back up, and the sun is still only a crescent in the sky growing imperceptibly. We can feel the heat returning; my jacket is uncomfortable and I take it off and drape it over a cedar stump.

Down on the roadway, a hundred yards from us, some teenagers have set up a large cardboard box with a cut out reflector made of aluminum foil so that they can safely observe the phases of the sun's return. I feel a remote pride in these kids even though I don't know them and can claim no part in their education or behavior. Not only are they being careful about their eyesight, but they have also gone to the trouble of setting up what amounts to be a small but clever (and inexpensive) astronomical observation post. But I am not distracted long from my original worries.

"So, what do you think happened to the horses?" I ask Lucinda.

"Let's go look," she says like the good sport she is.

So we amble back down the hill, past the pasture area, across another small wooded section, and there they are contentedly eating grass by the side of the road! When the sun was eclipsed, they assumed it to be evening and headed toward the roadway where they would generally be picked up by their owners and led to a more secure place. But the night had passed quickly and now they were back to their grazing, but staying close to the pick-up area just in case.

Lucinda did not hear them move away in the darkness. Since she was only a few feet way, I must assume that they neither whinnied nor galloped. They simply walked quietly to their evening pick-up stop. Similarly, the birds (except for a few vociferous crows early on) did not appear to do anything unusual during the eclipse. They grew quieter in the dark, especially the song birds. Other than that, there is no odd behavior to report.

Perhaps the most interesting thing has been the behavior of the Mexican young people. They cheered in joyous solidarity, and then went about the business of making careful observations. This to me shows both spiritual health (wonderment and joy) and intellectual vitality (utilization of scientific devices and close observation) which bodes well for the future of this part of the American continent.

It wasn't always that way of course. Aztec tradition held that eclipses were part of an eternal battle between day and night. At some point in these conflicts the god of night would begin to devour the sun. Human sacrifice was one way to propitiate the gods.

The Aztecs also believed that unborn children would suffer birth defects during those times when the sun was totally or partially eclipsed. In order to protect themselves, pregnant women would tie a piece of flint around their necks. The custom later changed to tying a red ribbon around the stomach, or the wearing of red clothing. In contemporary Mexico, indigenous people—especially in the Mexico City area— still do this. Other pregnant mothers wear a small piece of metal (usually a key ring) around their waists. Many farmers continue to believe that their crops will be stunted or completely shriveled by the action of the eclipse.

We will read later in the newspapers that thousands of indigenous people refused to come out of their homes during the eclipse. Fearful and troubled, the men had put red ribbons on stakes around their corn fields the night before, locked their doors, put blankets on the windows. The women wrapped chains of aluminum poptop rings around their waists, and then sat out the crucial time in their bedrooms.

But right now we are here, present, filled with this moment. We feel no fear, only a simple wonder despite our readings and our knowledge. And gratitude. How wonderful it is to be alive at this exact place in the solar system, to witness this remarkable event.

The thunder has ceased rattling in the distance. The sun is shining more and more brightly. When we look again through the protective windows of the welder's masks we see an image which looks like the famous BatSignal which the Caped Crusader would project on the sky to let Robin or the Chief know where he was. It is a lemon yellow bat wing which grows slowly into a three-quarter sun. Holy Helios, Batman! Leaping Luminosities!

2:05 PM It is time to rest before the alliterations (Tom Swifties to be precise) get worse. Time to make some notes, and enjoy our picnic lunch. Lucinda and I hug each other silently and kiss, like other lovers must be doing somewhere else in the woods, not needing or wanting a private darkness; shameless under the newborn sun.

ANOTHER REASON FOR LOVING FATHERS

In every darkened room there are unseen presences which (as one slips from the bonds of consciousness) assert themselves. They crawl like shadowy, unattached tentacles across the bedstead; they hover beneath the creaking floorboards waiting until you are taken by sleep (death's sweet companion) into the other world where they descend wrapped around the contours of your teeming brain.

For the brain never sleeps—we know. It simply flows from one world to the next, and one world is neither more nor less real than the other. We become inured by maturity, by the tales of reassuring fathers, of gentle protective fathers, our confidence in their voices stronger than the spirits which surround us. Through endless, reasonable repetition they assure us that these presences do not exist. There is no beast in the closet, no monster under the bed, no vampire lurking outside the window.

A father myself, I reassured my three-year-old daughter when she tenaciously held on to me and refused to go to sleep. I opened her closet to reveal a rumpled coat, not a witch. I pushed the broom under her bed. And, even after such tedious monster-proofing, she would still not go to sleep, unless the bedside lamp was left burning brightly. Wise child.

Some years later, working as a volunteer counselor in the alcoholic ward at San Francisco General Hospital, I was rushed to the bedside of a man in the chronic ward suffering from delirium tremens.

"The snakes! The snakes! Don't let them get me!" he screamed, kicking the covers off the bed, crawling into a corner of the room, naked, gasping for breath, his eyes bulging with fear, heart racing, adrenalin pumping.

I buzzed for the on-call doctor but, when he finally arrived ten minutes later, after the non-existent snakes had bit the patient repeatedly with their non-existent heart-stopping venom, the man was dead. The patient, who had no previous history of heart disease, had suffered massive cardiac arrest. He had no defense against the monsters.

In the same hospital a year later, a businessman was admitted who had suffered a stroke. The man had lived a very successful life. He had prospered in business, owned a lovely house, and had two children in private schools. He was respected by his neighbors and his colleagues. Yet, in his distant past he had a memory.

One day when he was a teenager, coming home from a party, he crashed his father's car. Beside him, carefully seat-belted, was his girlfriend. As they rounded a turn, too fast for the wet and slippery conditions of the two-lane mountain road, the car slid off the pavement, down an embankment and crashed into a tree. His girlfriend, jerked violently forward and then back by the collision, broke her neck. When he recovered consciousness, his first vision was that of her face, horrified in death, her head twisted all the way around to her back, staring at him with a rictus grin.

After his stroke, his brain became frozen in that particular synaptic sequence which was recorded at the age of sixteen. It played that vision—of his girlfriend in the family car, looking at him over and over and over—every minute of every day as he grimaced and slurred with horror in the prison of his hospital room.

There are no monsters under the bed.

"Now I lay me down to sleep," the child prays trustingly. And so we reassure the child. But the second half of the old prayer we no longer say—it seems too morbid, too medieval—"if I die before I wake, I pray the Lord my soul to take." But the soul is not so easily given up to the Lord. The soul, the synaptical wiring which charges the body we so trustfully lay to rest each evening, is alive with terrible things to do, and it does them even after the body is still.

Even now as the shadows fall, and the curtains rustle in the night breeze, even now as the branches scratch against the window panes, some loving father will tell his daughter that old lie, "There are no monsters," and then return to his own bed and breathe a true and silent prayer: May your mind be as a dwelling place for all sweet sound and harmonies, and when the monsters come—as indeed they will at 4 a.m. in some far off land where you lie alone in a strange bed—may they find no room, no room at all, my beautiful daughter, in the mansion you have built there.

JUDAS BURNING

Here in Guadalajara the roses bloom all year, even in the dry season when the dust tastes of burning carcasses and excrement. Purple jacaranda blossoms appear in the trees, and bougainvillea covers the broken glass of the high walls of the wealthy houses in Colonia Seatle. What we depend upon is not illusion but the generous paradox of dry arroyos and night-blooming acacia, the fresh fruit and flowers sold by local women, the blanketed Indians in the tropical heat, a place where Christ bleeds darkly and the Virgin is bright with victory candles.

I have left Barrio Padre for the long walk up the cobblestone streets to the Basilica. It is not exactly a holiday or a fiesta. It is merely Thursday of Holy Week and yet the square is crowded with Huichol Indians dressed in blues, oranges, startling pinks and purples. There are stands selling roasted corn on the cob, hot corn tortillas, baked *empanadas* filled with strawberry, or the *tuna* fruit of the cactus. I have come here thinking of attending Mass (there is one every hour) and yet the Basilica is packed at ten o'clock and again at eleven after I've made my leisurely circuit of the square.

There are Judas dolls for sale, ugly little things with straw bodies. Their faces remind me of Miss Piggy, although none are as cute. There is something unholy about these dolls, like those used in witchcraft or voodoo.

A priest has come out of the side door of the Basilica and the crowd gathers around him as he reads from the Bible. The noise of the hawkers and buyers, children and dogs, has quieted mysteriously. One has the feeling of being in two worlds here. The ancient Basilica with its wooden floors and bleeding Christ, its crumbling wall and footworn stone steps seems to belong to another Church more ancient and terrible than that indicated by the modern sculpture in front which depicts mild Pope John visiting Mexico and blessing Zapopan.

Someone begins shaking seeds in a hollow gourd and others join in with wooden rattles (which are for sale) as the priest reads from the Bible. "Because Judas knew the place, and brought a band of men and officers from the chief priests, with lanterns, torches and weapons..."

And now Judas comes, carried by two Huicholes with bleached white cotton pants held up by ropes for belts, their naked chests gleaming wetly bronze in the noonday sun. Their Judas is a straw man in a costume of colored feathers with a gruesome pig's face. He looks through the trees for the Savior. He looks through the crowd and the people raise their hands to block his view. To the side of the crowd are some white and red oleander bushes. This is where the figure of Christ has been hidden all along.

More Huichol men stand in front of the bushes very quietly. They could be anywhere. Outside an adobe hut in Puebla, in front of a liquor store in Tucson. They look like they have been here in this spot forever. They do not wish to attract attention. They are as part of the landscape. *Horseman, pass by!* But it is precisely this spot that Judas approaches. He is interested in what is behind those bushes. The sound of the seeds in the gourd and the sound of the rattles increase in volume.

The ugly pigfaced Judas is carried through the poisonous oleander bushes to where the statue of Christ is hidden. The priest intones: "He has given them the sign that whosoever he shall kiss, that is the Savior." And the straw effigy of Judas is borne by the two barechested Indians to the Christ statue. The priest reads on: "And Jesus says to the soldiers, 'Whom do you seek?' They reply, 'Jesus of Nazareth.' And the Savior says, 'I am He whom thou seeketh.'"

Then the effigy of Judas is carried to a side street. It is strung up with the help of some young boys and suspended from an ash tree. And, if Jesus is to have his hand-painted sign "Jesus of Nazareth, King of the Jews" at the hour of his crucifixion, Judas also will be acknowledged. Hastily-written signs appear on his chest and back: "Foreign Debt," names of dishonest politicians, "Yanquis Asesinos." Judas is more than a symbol. He is the embodiment of all the betrayals suffered and those still to be suffered. A young woman hangs a sign with the name of a lover who abandoned her. On a whitewashed wall nearby are faded red letters: *"PUTO BUSH CREE QUE UN LITRO DE GASOLINA VALE UN MUNDO DE SANGRE."* A not-so-subtle reference to the Gulf War which was not so popular here as it appeared to be further North.

Then someone approaches with a burning stick soaked in kerosene and proceeds to set fire to the effigy of Judas. It burns for a moment or two and then explodes with a startling POOM! scattering cloth, straw and colored paper over the crowd.

Then children with their doll-sized Judases dance around. And young men holding other Judases on long poles stuffed with fireworks set them on fire. The crowd shouts and chants, the seeds in the gourds rattle like evil snakes, and everywhere the dogs are barking and howling.

Frances Calderón de la Barca, witnessing a scene similar to this in Mexico City in the last century, was appalled at the "ugly misshapen monsters" representing Judas which filled the *Semana Santa* streets. "Poor Judas," she wrote. "Did he ever dream then that in the lapse of ages his effigies should be held up to the desecration of an unknown people in an undiscovered country beyond the sea? A secret bargain, perhaps made whisperingly in a darkened chamber with fierce Jewish rulers; but now shouted forth in the ears of the descendants of Montezuma and Cortés."

I am reminded of another Holy Week when, broke and living in a cheap hotel in San Francisco, I read the Chekhov story in which a young man hears again the story of Simon Peter's denial of Christ during a reading of the Passion at his local church. So moved is he that he relates it to a peasant woman he meets in the village on his way home. And, as he retells the story with "the enthusiasm of one who has understood it clearly for the first time," the peasant woman begins to weep. The young man weeps as well.

The young man is struck suddenly by the durability of the story and its accessibility. It has moved both him, an educated youth, and this unlettered peasant. Separated from each other by an enormous gulf, distanced by culture and the ages from the Jewish fisherman, they are still able to weep in empathy for Peter as he denies knowledge of his Lord not once, but "three times before the cock crowed."

What grief he must have felt, this Simon! What remorse must have filled his heart; how heavy and empty his life must have seemed then. He, like Judas, had clearly betrayed his master ("I do not know the man!").

So, why is Simon, now Peter, the "rock" of the Church, while Judas is a figure of universal condemnation? One a saint and the other buried in unhallowed ground? Why is one enshrined and the other vilified if they both committed the same crime: betrayal of a friend and teacher?

Peter, hearing the cock crow, "went out and wept bitterly." Judas "repented himself and... cast down the thirty pieces of silver saying, 'I have sinned in that I have betrayed innocent blood.'" Clearly they both felt remorse. Clearly they both acknowledged their crimes and repented. Moreover, Judas actually went and made amends, returning the money he had received.

If there is any difference in these men it would seem only to have been Judas' despair. For Simon lived with his shame, his remorse, hoping against hope. Judas, on the other hand, "having cast down the silver pieces, departed, and went and hanged himself."

One of my favorite stories is when Christ returns from the dead and appears to the Apostles. He called Peter to him. "Simon," he says, "lovest thou Me?" "Yea, Lord," says Peter. "You know I love You." Jesus says, "Feed my sheep." A second time Jesus asks, "Lovest thou Me?" Again Peter replies, "You know I do, Lord." "Feed my sheep," says Jesus.

A third time Jesus asks, "Simon, lovest thou Me?" "Yea, Lord," says Peter, who by now must have gotten the point. "You know I love You." Jesus says to him, "Feed my lambs."

Denied by his friend three times in succession, Jesus forgives him three times, contingent on an affirmation of love also made three consecutive times. Some divine humor there! But also an echo of his own teaching to forgive "even unto seventy times seven times."

Then finally he says to Simon: "I say unto thee thou art Peter and upon this rock I will build my Church." A pun on *petrus* (more humor) and another echo, for Jesus had promised earlier that in his kingdom "the last shall be first." Peter thus receives an unearned promotion from the ranks of the twelve apostles. Unearned grace. Unearned forgiveness. Exactly what Judas in his materialistic mind-set refused. Return of the thirty pieces of silver, yes. But he followed that by a negation of hope. Refusing to believe in forgiveness, he took his life.

Peter gave nothing but his persistent "Yea!" in the face of Jesus's questions. But these "yeas" were extensions of the earlier affirmation when, full of remorse, self-pity, self-hatred and angst, he did not give in to despair but held on when there was little to hope for except "the belief in things unseen," the power of love which would eventually redeem him.

When Judas is taken in effigy from the Zapopan plaza, he is more than a symbol. He is the dry straw of all the betrayals we have suffered which clogs the drainage of our hearts, which fills our mouth with the taste of rancid wine and the dust of tombs. All the betrayals, the bitterness, the resentments which must be burned away if we are ever truly to live again, ever to be reborn.

A few months ago Texas executed still another convicted felon. After the execution reporters asked the mother of the murder's victim if, now that the man was dead, she could forgive him. "Never," she said. "I will never forgive him as long as I live." I wish she could have been here today.

The sibilant strains of the *Miserere* in the evening echo among the emptying fruit stands and the stalls of the vendors. I buy a cup of cut melon and begin walking home. There has not been a single church bell rung in all of Mexico today. And there will not be until Easter morning. It had not occurred to me how much I would miss that. The deep and unutterable sadness of someone used to being lulled to sleep by the sound of foghorns or the lapping of waves now alone in the silent night of the high plateau of Jalisco. Hard to believe that the Resurrection is less than three days away. A small taste perhaps of what Judas felt.

FORT ADAMS

Before the Jazz Festivals, the condominiums, the gentrification of Thames Street, the Bed and Breakfasts, and the construction of the bridge that let the tourists and New York investors turn my hometown into a theme park, there was another Newport. Shrouded by fog, slowed by cobblestone streets, full of abandoned mysterious mansions, turreted and dark, it was a town that held history as mysteriously as the true wine in some misplaced medieval Grail.

It was in this town at the unreflecting age of twelve that I travelled with my best buddy Tommy by bicycle up the broad stretch of Harrison Avenue headed for the Ocean Drive. Our destination was an old fort, long-abandoned, which looked out over cliffs above Narragansett Bay, guarding the entrance to the harbor.

It was a place where we were forbidden to go. Honeycombed with flooded tunnels in danger of imminent collapse, the ten-acre fort was full of unexploded ordnance, of rusted ammunition, broken pipes, and empty buildings where sailors on shore leave (it was said) took unsuspecting virgins, and where escaped convicts had in fact been tracked down and, soaked by fog and rain and cold, surrendered peacefully to the law.

On this particular day in October, when the fog lay heavy on the roads, we cut off to the dirt path bordered by knee-high, seed-scattering weeds, feeling the salt dew soak our pants and the gonad-smashing

bike seats setting puberty back a year. We suffered it all, as good soldiers would, because we were planning a defensive attack on the am-
phibious German force which even now was steaming up the harbor
threatening the town.

When we reached the parade ground of the old fort we cut saplings
and pretended they were M-1's. We paraded for a bit under my orders
either because Tommy was less argumentative, or because (as I believed)
the leadership qualities of the Irish were inimitable. Then I gave the
order that the M-1's were now Thompson sub-machine guns, far more
satisfying weapons, capable of annihilating whole platoons as we set off
through darkened half flooded tunnels, clotted with debris of old storms
and vandals, and killed the Germans who had already come ashore in
black rubber boats and who were, from the ugly grimaces as their faces
contorted in rictus of death, stopped in the nick of time from attacking
our sisters. Terrible, black-shirted, lightning-epauleted Nazis quickly
dispatched to the world of Hades, so now we rested with army can-
teens of Kool-Aid and stolen Camels and Old Golds and planned our
next assault.

At the highest point of the fort was a cannon emplacement called
Battery O'Shea. Overgrown with weeds, its old rusted gun founda-
tions were mounted on top of a grass-covered hill. The hill was deceiv-
ing, however, because it was hollow. Inside was an empty ammunition
park, big as a airplane hanger, which could be accessed by a rusted iron
door six feet high. We discovered that if we both pulled on the door
together, our combined strength served to get it open. And, in the process
of opening, the rusted hinges let forth a moanful sound that echoed
out over the Bay like a foghorn.

Picture us then, planning our next attack. The German fleet coming up to the entrance of the Bay. We, the local rangers, having taken
out the advance troop, now sending signals to the American destroyers
in the harbor. We climbed up on the seats of our bikes so that we could

both hang from the iron door and swing it together. Oooom-oooom, the deep-throated voice bellowed out of the eerie fog over the hill and across the cold waters. Each time we swung, the heavy door gained momentum and on the third pass, Tommy fell off and the door continued forward with only me aboard and my thumb hanging off the far side where it was sliced by the rusted metal of the doorjam and blood jetted out like that of a bullfighter caught in the artery by a horn. I dropped to the ground, too stunned by what had happened to feel pain, but sickened when I saw the white flash of bone beneath the skin and the scrap of flesh that was once my thumb hanging down in a wet flap.

Tommy, with an instinct true to the breed of summer soldiers and sunshine patriots, or perhaps just fearful that he would be blamed, jumped on his bike and took off down the hill. I reached in my pocket and took out the handkerchief I always carried (one of three things a gentleman always had, my father counseled—I forget the other two), wrapped the wound tight and mounted my bike. The ride home, about a mile or so, was one of panic because my pants were soaked by wet grass, my shirt covered in blood, and the injury surely in need of some outside attention which would mean a trip to our nearsighted local sawbones whose ministrations were as painful as most injuries.

But beneath all this, or perhaps on top of it, was the slowly lifting fog, the splash of color in the harbor as the sun threw its sparkling mantle across the bay, the cool drip-soaked rush beneath the elm trees, and the feeling—not terrible just desolate—that I was alone. I was alone with my pain, with the blood, the white bone, the jet spray of my heart pump as my skinny legs pedaled the Schwinn Green Hornet home. Tommy had left me through panic and fear. And even home, the place that I headed, because there was no other place close by, would—I suspected—not be one of solace or sympathy. Punished once by the fates, I would be drubbed again by Mom for breaking rules, ruining

my clothes, and racking up still another doctor's bill. Alone, alone, the
outlaw child.

The feeling passed quickly. By the time I turned in to the gravel
drive of the white cottage I called home, the tears were already stream-
ing down my face. Fantasizing that I would lose my thumb, that I
would die from blood loss, helped me in the performance which was
calculated to avoid a beating.

"What happened NOW!" my mother shouted as I staggered into
the kitchen."

"I got hurt, up at Battery O'Shea…"

"Blood, blood!" she shouted as I stood there dripping through my
improvised bandage. "All over my just-waxed floor. Over to the sink
with that mess, you…" she snatched me by the shoulder. "And just
what were you doing at that place? I've told you and told you, time and
time again…"

"We were just playing and…"

"Was there rust?" she said. "Was there rust on what cut you?"

"Yes. But why…"

"Oh Jesus, Mary and Joseph. Lockjaw! You just wait here."

She called my father at work and together they took me to the half-
blind octogenarian doctor. My father was silent and grim, while my
mother continued regaling me the whole way with descriptions of the
horrible death caused by blood poisoning where the jaw locks tight and
the patient dies in spastic convulsions strangling on his own tongue.

We rushed into the doctor's office where he was roused from his
midmorning nap. Grouchy and maladroit, he proceeded to clean the
wound, give me a dozen stitches, a tetanus shot, all of which proce-
dures caused far more pain than the accident itself.

"Why do you DO these things to me?" wailed my mother as the
doctor drew his thick needle with catgut through my torn flesh. "Why…
to me?"

"You cause your mother a great deal of misery, boy," said the doctor, grunting as he hit bone, and then pulled the needle out for a second go at it.

"Oww!" I cried out, the tears welling despite my intent to be stoic.

I felt like telling him to pay attention to his work and not be distracted by my mother's hysterics. But the two of them were getting along fine. It was almost as if they were enjoying it.

"Ah, you think THAT hurts, do you? Well, think of the pain your mother's had to put up with. First when you were born...

"Oh, do you remember, doctor?" my mother said. "Eight hours in labor and finally the caesarean."

"I remember it well. During a blackout it was. Generators wouldn't kick in. And there was this bucko headed out sideways. He almost killed you, no doubt of it."

"And then the chicken pox," added my mother, warming up now that she had a sympathetic ear. "The mumps, the fall from the garage roof when he was pretending to fly, the accident with the knife when he thought he was Jim Bowie, stepping on a broken bottle at the beach, crashing his bike into the tractor trailer... Why does he DO these things to me?"

"He's a trial, no question there," the doctor said, giving the knot in the last stitch a final vicious twist. "Seems like he's made it his life's work to make you miserable."

We walked to the car and my father put his arm around me.

"You know your mother is easily upset, son. Why do you do these things to her?"

Jesus, I thought. From him, too. Is everyone crazy here? I was the one that got hurt. I was the one who was abandoned by my friend. I was the one whose hand was used as a practice quilt by a purblind geriatric. Doing things to HER! Give me a break.

"Listen," I said. "I don't suppose I could have a cigarette."

"Jesus, Mary, and Joseph!" my mother said, coming out the door just as I made my ill-timed request. "Cigarettes! What next? Even the prodigal son was repentant."

I was quiet on the way home. Drained I supposed of tears, of blood, of any hope of being understood, of even receiving sympathy. They didn't give kids pain pills in those days, and the local anesthetic had worn off halfway though the stitching procedure, so I was feeling kind of bad. But below this pain, the throbbing ache in my hand, the weakness, the nausea, was that desolation again. Sitting in the back seat of that '52 Plymouth, breathing in the sick car smell of stale cigarette smoke from my father's Old Golds and the even sicker odor of the Lily of the Valley perfume my mother wore, I felt alone. How could I even be related to these people? What was I even doing in this town? I didn't belong here. I was alone, a stranger, a creature who somehow or another appeared here, brushed against people, but was not really one of them. Alone. Alone. And I knew then that I would always be. Oh, I would learn to get along well enough, and sometimes, assuming a virtue that I did not have, would come close to connecting. But even behind the most cherished friendship, the most genuine love, was that cold fog, the drip from the elm trees, the desolation. At first it was a place I fled from, sometimes in sports, sometimes in drink, sometimes in marathon conversations with poets that lasted until dawn. But it became a place I could not truly escape.

Every tree, Rilke once wrote, is the first tree of one's childhood. As a writer I have learned to return to that place, not in fear and trembling anymore, but in expectation that like the desert cactus which holds in its century of solitude the promise of a white blossom, this place is also the truest one for me, the place where all trivia is stripped away and what is left is steady pulse of gestation. I have learned that not only will this gestation not kill me (as my earlier one apparently almost killed my mother) but will with its monsters and its angels pull me from myself so that I can become new again.

When the poet William Stafford died a few years ago, I went back and reread all his work. He was an accessible and kindly poet whose words continue to inform the best part of my literary memories. But of all these poems this gentle soul wrote, the one that seems most cold, most desolate, is also the one that also feels truest to me, and I suspect gave him the lever with which he moved us all. It's called "Ask Me."

Some time when the river is ice ask me
mistakes I have made. Ask me whether
what I have done is my life. Others
have come in their slow way into
my thought, and some have tried to help
or to hurt: ask me what difference
their strongest love or hate has made.

I will listen to what you say.
You and I can turn and look
at the silent river and wait. We know
the current is there, hidden, and there
are comings and goings from miles away
that hold the stillness exactly before us.
What the river says, that is what I say.

LETTER TO A TROUBLED STUDENT

Dear Willie,

Last week in class when we were discussing the Indian[1] uprising in Chiapas, I mentioned the international movement of indigenous people following the Columbus Tri-centenial and the growing violence which has been blossoming all over the Americas. I had in mind the massacre of the prison inmates by the Venezuelan Indians last week, the street violence of the Canadian Indians last year, the outbreaks of violence in Guatemala, and the property seizure and postings of the Mohawks in the Adirondacks. I said it was scary.

Your response was, "Why is it scary? They only want what is theirs, and they were here first." I don't know if my response was a sensitive one or if it came from being a teacher at an elitist school and a part of the middle class. I do know that my answer was partial—and as such half true and half false.

I said that just because a culture existed in the 1600s did not mean

---

1. I'm aware that political correctness in the United States has substituted the word Native American for Indian. The term *indio* is more common in Mexico where I live and where the Indians are not native to the United States of America. Since "American" is of European derivation anyway, "Native American" seems absurd when applied to indigenous peoples whether in Mexico or the United States. Nevertheless, I apologize to anyone who is offended.

the culture had survived, or that the descendants of that culture had the right to use violence against the rest of us. The example I gave was of the Irish Republican Army, which had been bombing civilians in London to force the British government to return Northern Ireland to them. It is scary to think that innocent children are killed and maimed in the streets of London because some Irishman feels this is the only way he can fight for part of his lost homeland.

Yet, it is clear to him that there is no other way. An Irish army would be quickly crushed by an English one. Just as a Mohawk army would be easily crushed by an American one. For a minority to claim back what was theirs historically after they have lost the power to do so, means they must rely on terrorism, frightening the ordinary innocent people through random violence in the hope that the dominant government will make concessions. That is scary.

It is easy for some of us—such as yourself— to take the Indians' side. They did lose their land, unfairly, solely as a result of the superior and often ruthless force of the Anglo. But remember the Anglo also took Arizona, California, New Mexico, Wyoming, and parts of Colorado and Kansas from the Mexicans in the same way. How would you feel if you were living in San Francisco, and a bunch of Mexican terrorists tried to reclaim their land by blowing up the Golden Gate Bridge and killing any Anglos whom they happened to encounter, as well as any Japanese, Chinese, Greeks and Chileans who happened to be driving across? Scared? Or would you simply say, "What's the big deal? It was their land first." And remember Mexicans were just robbed of their territory 150 years ago and they were a recognized Republic—their claims would be more recent and, at least under the laws which govern republics, more persuasive under international law.

I also wonder—not as a teacher and defender of the status quo—but as a student of history, if this generation of Americans such as yourself might have been fed too heavy a dose of minority propaganda, not tempered by real history. Read, for example, of the savageries of the Apache against their neighboring tribes. The slaughters of the peace-loving Maricopa. Or the murders of women and children in the Pima tribe by their indigenous neighbors. I don't think I need to point out the thousands of skulls that Cortéz encountered in New Spain, or the bloodletting and human sacrifices of the beautiful Aztec culture.

If the remainder of the tribes could get their territories back, would we really like to see the return of these cultures? Would the smaller Indian tribes even like to see it? I don't think we really have to worry about that, though. In those few cases where old treaties have been acknowledged, tribes in the southwest and northeast, for example, have chosen to claim their exemption from local laws by opening gambling casinos on Indian lands to rake in millions of dollars from tourists, thus embracing the worst of the dominant culture.

I also think—as a human being this time—not as your teacher, or as a historian—but just as a person— that no matter what happens, we will lose and the Indians will lose. Life is more complicated than any pro-Indian or anti-Indian stance allows us to admit. We both know what happens in *When Legends Die* and we both know that it is much different and much more complex than any polemic about white men and Indians. It is about all of us as people, the complications our history has made, how we come to terms with them as individuals.

My concern is, first of all, life. Anyone shooting guns at anyone else is scary to me, whether the reason is pursuit of drugs or pursuit of happiness. Revolutions are, more often than not, simply bloodbaths in which innocent people get killed and in which the so-called freedom obtained turns out to be nothing more than a different set of bosses running the same old show. Again, look at history.

I think books—especially novels such as *When Legends Die*— are more important than guns because they have the power to transform us as human beings. Because no matter what side you take in this question of the indigenous peoples vs. the Europeans, the fact is that the truth is far too complex to ever unravel. And even if you could do it, you would still not find the solution, because the world would have already changed again away from the solution you had proposed. The Mexican soldiers fighting against the tribes in Chiapas are not followers of Cortéz. They themselves are the sons of Indians and Spaniards who have made their compromises and their sacrifices to live in peace and raise their children in this land. The truth will not be revealed in politics or taking sides. The truth is composed of paradoxes, ironies and contradictions, which are best understood in reading narratives like the one we shared in class. Beyond these there is failure of the imagination, reductionism, oversimplification, fundamentalism, fascism. That is what scares me as a human being. And I am not afraid for myself. I am afraid for you and the young people I teach who might be tempted to turn away from the possibilities of illumination and healing in the complexities of literature. That you might accept instead the easy answer of rhetoric or war, where either someone shoots someone else, and our guns are bigger than your guns, or someone shoots off his mouth: my father is better than yours. It is same old bullshit that has clogged this world in bloodbath after bloodbath throughout the centuries and taken us giant steps backward for every tiny step our thinking and writing have brought us out of the darkness.

The poet William Stafford once said,"The signals we give to each other should be real. The darkness around us is deep." William Stafford died this year; he is a part of that darkness now. I am not scared of it and am ready to go when it is my turn. But what I am afraid of is that the light which the human intellect has brought to this planet, and which I tend carefully in my classes, in my writings and in my life as if it were (and I believe it is) a sacred flame, will flicker out because men in search of redress for ancient grievances, or personal power, polarize nations in the Americas so that we become part of the insanity of Bosnia,

or Palestine, or Iraq, or Northern Ireland. You have not seen families
ripped apart by wars as I have. Not just the friends and family members
that died, but those that lived not speaking to each other because they
had opposite views, or those that ended up in insane asylums because
they could not stand to remember what they did in the name of their
flag.

You have not seen a war yet. But you have seen a country who can't
take care of its homeless, or get health care for its poor, spend billions
of its gross national product on missiles. You have seen a country which
can't provide an affordable wage to a third of its people spend 40% of
its tax revenues on defense.

What a horror if Mexico, just now beginning to leave the Third
World behind (in part because of its 75 years of peace), just beginning
to have a prosperous middle class, just beginning to make real inroads
in feeding its poor, what a tragedy if this country which now spends
less than 10% of its GNP on defense would be forced to take money
which could be spent on making this a prosperous nation and divert it
instead to put down insurrection in its southernmost state, defend
against indigenous incursions along the Guatemalan border, buy planes
and weapons, and support a large standing army. That is scary. To think
that the 190 years since its independence, spent in evolving a national
state which finally is about to bear fruit, could be shattered and re-
gressed by a group of fanatics (justified as they may be in their ancient
grievances) is scary.

I guess that's all I had to say about it being scary. It was more than
I could say in class. It's not about who is right and who is wrong. We
are all partly right and all partly wrong. It's about how we can live
together and avoid killing each other; about how we can preserve human life and human intelligence. I am no flag waver—either for the
U.S. or for Mexico. I am not an Anglo-Saxon or Mexican so I don't
even have the racial ties to the dominant culture on either side of the

border. But I know about wars, and armies, and revolutions, and history, and death. And I know that in every war, truth is the first victim. And that's very scary.

Sincerely,

Your friend and teacher.

SAVAGE CAPITALISM

A Review of *Liberation and Development: A Latin American Perspective* by Fr. James Fogarty.

December of 1994 marked the winter of discontent in Mexico. The house of cards assembled by Carlos Salinas collapsed and the Mexican economy went spinning into the void. It was just eleven months after the much touted NAFTA agreement had been signed and "free trade" made its debut in Mexico.

Not at all coincidentally, the Zapatista Liberation Movement (EZLN) also came into existence eleven months earlier. The same day, in fact, that the NAFTA treaty was signed, a directive from Sub-Comandante Marcos was sent from the jungles of Chiapas. To the Zapatistas, as to many Mexicans, NAFTA spelled trouble from the start. Whole sections of industry would be faced with bankruptcy, they warned, profits would end up in the hands of the few, the rich would get richer, the poor poorer, and foreigners would be calling the shots.

For Father James Fogarty, a Catholic missionary working in the barrios of Mexico City, it was clear that the new order of unfettered capitalism had provoked a poverty crisis. Mexico, forced by the "free trade" agreement to stop protection of its domestic industries, to buy more U.S. imports, to pay debts to U.S. banks with a decreasing number of dollars, would do so at the expense of the poor by cutting back funds allocated for social services and domestic growth.

In the first eleven months of NAFTA Mexico had chalked up a $12 billion trade deficit. The Salinas regime created 22 new billionaires but Mexico's poorest group, unable to afford the basic *canasta*, or market basket, of food staples, had grown from 14 million to 21 million. Now in the winter of 1994, the new president, Ernesto Zedillo, had inherited the whirlwind. On December 21st the peso fell from 3.40 to the dollar to 6.50. The Bolsa, or Mexican stock market, dropped 12%. The Mexican meltdown had begun and Zedillo scrambled for help. Those who would bail him out were those who put his country in hot water in the first place, but there was no where else to go.

The U.S. and the International Monetary Fund came to the rescue. But the $52 billion dollar bailout ($20 billion from the U.S.) would carry a price. Loss of autonomy, a shameful lien on the patrimony of Mexican petroleum (only Saddam Hussein has been similarly humiliated by the U.S.), and increased poverty for Mexican people. "In effect," notes Fogarty, "the masses who did not contract the debts were condemned to suffer the austerity measures imposed by foreign creditors. These measures included drastic cutbacks in public spending and social services, so that a greater percentage of the GNP could be set aside for foreign debt servicing and repayment."

The price of tortillas (the basic Mexican comestible) rose 100% in the first 24 months of the crisis. According to a study conducted by Banamex, half of the Mexican population had a caloric intake below the U.N. minimum nutritional standard. Social programs were eviscerated; 22 billion dollars left Mexico in capital flight as the rich cashed in their chips. The poor were left to die in the streets, or take to the mountains and prepare for the coming revolution.

While Zedillo was eating tequila ice cream at his first White House reception and being complimented by fellow Yale alumnus Bill Clinton on his "bravery in the face of the economic crisis," Sub-Comandante Marcos was sending out missives via the internet that were appealing to the Mexican middle class. "This loan has been signed in... blood," he noted. While Clinton acknowledged much the same thing privately, he complimented Zedillo publicly on the "hard measures" he had imposed on the Mexican people in order to quickly repay the U.S. portion of the debt.

Free trade, NAFTA, foreign loans, economic "development" by First World nations, have resulted in "increased job insecurity, a rising crime rate, and growing social inequality," according to Fogarty. The Crisis of 1994 and its repercussions have simply expanded the field of victims to include "small and medium-sized business owners and employees, urban wage earners, women, rural communities and children." While the wealthy and middle class have seen some economic recovery since 1994, the poor have gotten poorer and funds intended for social services have been diverted to repay outstanding loans.

"Not without reason," continues Fogarty, "some Latin American critics of this latest version of laissez-faire capitalism are calling it *capitalismo salvaje* (savage capitalism) which in turn gives rise to what they call 'economic genocide' in the sense that it leads to the elimination of the poor who are superfluous to this economic model."

Fogarty, a proponent of liberation theology and social reform, calls for drastic changes in policies and structures which will allow the poor to become protagonists of their own emancipation from injustice and exploitation. Critical of the traditional role of the Catholic Church in Latin America, Fogarty calls for a new commitment to social change. He urges clergy and lay people alike to abandon the neo-capitalist and developmental policies which have ravaged Latin America, and work instead for "a more humanistic approach aimed at attacking the root causes of injustice, poverty and social unrest." He points out the success of alternative models such as Costa Rica, which reduced its poverty level by two-thirds in the difficult decade of the 1980s. The only other country which produced similar results, he notes, was Cuba, despite the economic restrictions imposed by its "neighbor" to the north.

It is clear that former President Bush's prediction in 1990 that the free-market system would bring peace and prosperity to Latin America has failed to materialize. What has resulted instead from NAFTA and increased foreign development is social unrest, increased unemployment, higher levels of poverty, and an unprecedented disparity of classes in the late 20th century. "It seems a fact of human experience," writes Fogarty, "that when peaceful evolution becomes impossible, violent resolution becomes inevitable." Fogarty is being heard in the hills of Guerrero, in the jungles of Chiapas, and in the *barrios* of Mexico City. One hopes he is listened to in the halls of government and the board rooms of industry as well. If not, his words may carry the historical weight of prophesy.

EDUCATION HELD HOSTAGE

The University is a place where inquiry is pushed forward, and discoveries verified and perfected, and rashness rendered innocuous, and error exposed, by the collision of mind with mind, and knowledge with knowledge.
— John Henry Newman

In the early morning hours of Sunday, October 6, 1999, when combined teams of crack commandos took control of the Autonomous University of Mexico (UNAM), the collision was far different from what Cardinal Newman foresaw in his "Idea of A University." The collision was not "mind with mind" or "knowledge with knowledge" but rather the concentrated force of the PFP (Policia Federal Preventiva) against a small group of young men and women. The order given by President Ernesto Zedillo the night before was intended to wrest control of the university from a group of striking students and professors and return it to the State by force.

The student strike at Latin America's largest university (approximately 200,000 students at the undergraduate, graduate and professional level) had paralyzed public education in Mexico's capital and frozen scientific research and social inquiry for the past ten months.

The strike had its origins in the March 19, 1999 decision of the University Council to raise tuitions across the board at the formerly free university. A week later there was a brief stoppage of university activities in protest, and three weeks later a full-scale strike and the basis for a political conflict in Mexico which continues to this day.

The original proposal was to raise university tuition for classes and services to better reflect the actual costs, and to accompany the increase with a program of loans and scholarships for needy students. The proposal, for those who are aware of the American model of higher education, does not seem radical. For Mexicans, however, it marked a decided change in the way which the country had done business since the Revolution. One of the rights established by the 20th century constitution which ended the Mexican Revolution was a right to free, public education for those qualified, and UNAM had become symbolic of that right. The transformation from this model into the two-tiered American model (those who can pay and those who cannot) appeared as a betrayal of that constitution and a movement away from education as a federally guaranteed right, to a class privilege for the few and public assistance for the remainder.

UNAM is host to a great deal of the country's technological, scientific, sociological and humanistic research. The bulk of its resources come from the federal government and are approved by the Congress. Only a small part of its funding (approximately $1.5 million) come from voluntary tuition and fees. As the protest movement grew and citizens turned against the proposed increases and sided with the students, the government launched an aggressive propaganda campaign against the protesters. The protesters were variously panned as kidnappers, rabble-rousers, Communists, leftist extremists, vandals and revolutionaries. While the Cold War may have ended with the demise of the USSR and the fall of the Berlin Wall, the rhetoric of that era is alive and well in Mexico and in most of Latin America. The political and military (police) machinery, the latter funded in part by the United States, have resulted in a variety of reformist movements to be labeled Communist, so that they could be combatted openly by the government or co-opted by official propaganda.

The original cause of the strike, the new tuition schedule, evolved as the strike progressed. The student strike committee also asked for a larger voice in terms of the university's government, the dissolution of links to private organizations, and democratic space within the university to discuss and resolve issues of the university's transformation in terms of research and management. It was these latter elements, not the tuition increase, which brought students and administrators to an impasse and ultimately resulted in the armed takeover of the university by the government.

It is worth noting that the student leaders saw the cause of the crisis as something much more than a simple tuition hike. They saw it another in a series of neoliberal, World Bank-inspired acts to eliminate public education in Latin America, and free the market for private educational investment. Their failure to clearly articulate this, however, lost them the support of the citizenry at a critical juncture.

Public education in Latin America has a different genesis and philosophy than that in the United States. The tradition of liberal arts, of humanistic research, of intellectual freedom (hence autonomous), and study of the social sciences which the U.S. has had since as early as 1638 with Harvard, and then later with Dartmouth, Yale, and other Ivy League and private universities has traditionally been the province of the autonomous but public university in Latin America. In the United States the land grant universities were instruments of the state, while the private universities were autonomous. In Latin America, the public university was autonomous while the private university, conversely, was tied to a religious or corporate agenda.

Now, with the neoliberal push in Latin America, the pressure is on the public universities to "compete" to "meet the demands of the market," which is to say, meet the demands of the business sector, and use their research facilities for the benefit of the private sector. In all cases

applied academics are favored over the theoretical. There is an impov-
erishment of intellectual debate and a narrowing of research agendas to
technical issues rather than broader social questions and problems. The
growing decline of funding for these universities has resulted in lower
salaries for professors, less space for classes, and limited or antiquated
facilities. As a result the private universities have taken a larger and
larger share of the market with all of the upper class students and most
of the middle class attending private universities. This privatization of
education has led in turn to the delegation of public responsibilities to
private institutions. As the Brazilian professor Pablo Gentili notes: "The
almost fundamentalist emphasis on the virtues of the market as the
most efficient avenue for capturing financial resources for teaching,
research and extension activities, not only challenges the role of the
state, but also enthrones mercantile and productivity-oriented criteria
in the allocation and distribution of public funds."

What does this mean in real terms to the people of Latin America
whose tax money is, without their knowledge, being reallocated in this
way? It means, according to Stanford's Center for Biomedical Ethics,
that diseases such as malaria, liver parasites and dengue fever which
affect public health in Latin America will not be funded by industry-
sponsored research because there is no profitability in the outcome. If
research is market-driven, then research into diseases which affect people in developing nations who can't afford to pay high prices for medi-
cine will not be pursued by the pharmaceutical industry. This is a clear
case of public funds being used for private industry contrary to the
public good.

In Mexico, it has recently been found that a new biologically-engi-
neered corn plant produces toxins which kill the Monarch butterfly.
The developer of the product is a biochemical company which had a
substantial part of the research and development of this product funded
by the public university system. The implications to Mexico in terms

of biological disruption, loss of natural resources, loss of tourism, destruction of natural beauty are enormous.

But let's return to the students and their dilemma. Assuming the university is back to business as normal, what is normal at this point? The inroads made by the private universities in hiring many of the best professors in the sciences, mathematics and technical disciplines, has left only a few dedicated people in these fields behind, along with the humanists who have no other home in the Mexican university system. Working in crowded classrooms, using outmoded facilities, they become more and more politicized. Since the humanities have become marginalized in the private universities where one's career must be chosen in the freshman year, the political theorists, the social scientists, the philosophers and writers are the inheritors of the abandoned autonomous institution. Their deep skepticism of the political process, their observation of the continuing economic crisis, their contempt of the so-called "rescues" of the country by the International Monetary Fund and the World Bank, their increasing marginalization in a nation which they feel has sold its birthright to the marketplace and exchanged constitutional privileges for the dollar, make them among the most radical thinkers in the country today. Likely enough their students are not only radical but probably the only thinkers in their age group because their contemporaries are too busy learning the minutiae of the new technology or the latest marketing agenda to have time to think. The students in private universities for the most part are too busy learning how to play the game to question whether the rules of the game are fair, or wise, or good for their country. The student strikers saw this clearly and it was part of the reason that the government viewed their protest as inherently dangerous and co-opted the media to transmit that message.

The protest was reduced by the government to the basic financial issue (the proposed tuition hike) in an ostensible attempt to resolve it.

However, the students who had observed the deterioration of higher public education while private education had prospered, who had witnessed the sacrifices of their parents as a result of government stabilization policies, who had seen the devaluation of the peso, the banking scandals, and were frustrated by a judicial system which favored the privileged, saw the obvious connection between these events and the privatization reforms proposed by the University Council. Now, even a freeze on tuition hikes would not be enough. The strike had reached an impasse.

The President made a nationally televised speech in which he expressed his hope that he could count on the support of the responsible middle class which had grown weary of lawlessness and a "university held hostage." He reminded his audience of the daily newspaper and television reports which clearly showed the government to be reasonable and the students to be adamant. He need not have worried. Most citizens in the Republic sat back in their living rooms and watched the (pre-recorded for prime time) carefully orchestrated seizure of the University installations by helmeted and jackbooted paramilitary forces operating under Presidential mandate. The forces retaking the university were unarmed, noted the President who was anxious to avoid a repeat of 1968 when several hundred students were massacred, but their number (in excess of 2,000) insured a minimum of resistance from the handful of students inside. Just in case, however, machine guns and M-16s were being held at port arms position by forces outside the university gates.

That said, however, it should be noted that the students themselves helped to contribute to the breakdown in negotiations. The leadership did not take into consideration the demands of the majority when a compromise was offered, they cordoned off the negotiation table with barbed wire, their attacks and contempt for the press was continual, and their insults and physical confrontations were a threat to public order. Nevertheless, this is just the sort of confrontational and authoritarian behavior they had seen from the government.

The lack of trust inherent in the political system, negative attitudes from citizens who objected to closing highways and research facilities, also tended to marginalize the student leadership further. It ended as might have been predicted: with the university in greater disarray, with the public university concept so tainted that many employers looking for university graduates now put "no UNAM need apply" in their ads, and with the neocapitalist star in the ascendent. Not an encouraging message to the social movements in Latin America in the future, watching constitutional rights disappear by executive mandate, and the largest university become a tool of the market-driven world economy.

This spring, as students come home from technical universities across Latin America, wired to the internet but encountering only the occasional professor, with their own webpage but a negligible library, their careers assured (as long as the skills they've learned are still required by the economy after they graduate) but with fewer and fewer programs in humanities, social sciences and arts and thus little idea of how their country is run or what might be done to change it, the words of Cardinal Newman seem anachronistic:

> The University... is the place to which a thousand schools make contributions; in which the intellect may safely range and speculate... It is the place where the professor becomes eloquent, displaying his science in its most complete and winning form, pouring it forth with the zeal of enthusiasm, and lighting up his own love for it in the breast of his hearers. It is the place which wins the admiration of the young by its celebrity, kindles the affections of the middle aged by its beauty, and rivets the fidelity of the old by its associations. It is the seat of wisdom, a light of the world, a minister of the faith, an Alma Mater of the rising generation.

Such *was* the idea of a university. The strike at UNAM and its aftermath have given us a clearer look at the future and the university that is to be. It is a vision of the future which is, at best, uncertain; at worse, bleak.

THE STREET PEOPLE OF JALISCO

There are few homeless people on the streets of Guadalajara. Mexican families tend to provide for even the most troublesome or feckless of their members. The extended family includes even distant cousins and it is considered shameful to have any relative, no matter how remote, not minimally provided for. Yet, during the daytime and early evening hours there are several groups of what one might, for lack of a better epithet, term "street people." However, since this generic phase is demeaning, I'll provide each group with the name most commonly used for them by the locals.

VENDEDORES DE CHICLE (Chewing gum Sellers). These are usually young Indian (Huichol) children, boys and girls from the ages of nine to twelve, who sell Adams Chiclets to the people in cars stopped at traffic lights. The children are often scantily clad: boys in ragged shorts with no shirts, girls in cheap but brightly colored polyester shifts. They are usually barefoot and occasionally dirty but, in spite of this, often possess a startling beauty. Their large eyes are black and luminescent like those of children in a De Gracia painting; their complexions are flawless and the color of ripening wheat, their bodies are doe-skin brown. Any one of these children picked at random could be the subject of a UNESCO poster ("Save The Children") which would melt the hardest heart.

Some people have told me that they never buy gum from these children. They say it just encourages the parents to keep them out on the street. Thus, they argue, each peso one provides helps underwrite a bad system. I disagree. The Indian mother can often be seen at the curb in the shade of a eucalyptus with a child at her breast. Sometimes she'll be preparing tortillas and beans (the afternoon meal) on the median strip. Often one sees indigenous mothers and fathers selling mats, basketwork, and other handicrafts on the side of the street opposite their children. The men are in dungarees, or cotton pants and t-shirts. The women are bundled up in several layers of clothing often including a woven *rebozo* wrapped around the shoulders. These women are thick, squat and prematurely aged, but they are out there working.

Young Indian females provide most of the cheap maid service to the Mexican middle class and upper class. Often they have live-in employment with the families they serve. However, this group of girls in their late teens and twenties have extended families. They have younger bothers and sisters, mothers, grandmothers and pregnant aunts who have accompanied them from the Indian village to the city and now must find some way to supplement the income of the lucky girl who has steady employment. Thus, the Chiclet vendors and the sellers of handicrafts. These family members often live in tin-and-cardboard makeshift houses at the edge of the city. Sometimes they commute at the end of the work week or on a feast day to their distant villages. But most of the time they are there in the city, to provide the protection, the unity, the traditions and values to the young girls of the family. Family unity is important. It is the predominant value in the Mexican world and is just as significant to the indigene as it is to the white or mestizo.

Hence the philosophy of not buying Chiclets as a way of refusing to support an unpleasant economic reality punishes the wrong people and cannot accomplish its purpose. The injustice began with Cortéz and the European exploitation of the Indians. The disruption of the indigene lifestyle continues with the Mexican middle class and tourist hotels pulling their supply of cheap domestic labor from the Indian villages. If my friends who choose not to buy Chiclets from the Indian children want to be consistent, they would also refuse laundry and maid service, as well as boycotting tourist hotels and condos.

LOS PAYASOS. (The Clowns). When the light turns red at the intersection of Avenida Hidalgo and Américas, ten-year-old Felipe and his teenage brother Carlos bound out into the street. There amid the cars, trucks and taxi cabs they do handstands, tumbles and cartwheels. Though underweight, they are both athletic and well-conditioned. They are dressed in baggy pants whose blue and white stripes are a little wider than those of mattress ticking or the pants worn by convicts in the Southern U.S, but identical to both in color and texture. The boys have identical red polo shirts, and the oldest sports a wide-brimmed straw hat. Each has a red bulb-like fake nose; each has white pancake makeup around the eyes and mouth. Carlos wear brown sandals; his little brother a pair of inexpensive but new tennis shoes.

Felipe jumps up on his brother's back. He almost loses his footing but then his brother squares his shoulders and, balanced precariously, the youngster juggles three orange tennis balls. This routine, amateurish but enthusiastic, lasts little more than a minute which leaves them less than thirty seconds to go by the driver's side of the waiting cars to collect their tips. Then the light changes and they jump quickly back onto the sidewalk to wait for the next opportunity.

When I ask about the police they both say that the cops are no problem. They are seldom bothered. They are not beggars, after all, and they do not annoy people. They simply provide a free show for the passing motorists. Those who are entertained and wish to tip the boys do so. The rest go about their business. It does not seem dangerous work to them and the pay is good. Felipe says that during the evening rush hour (5 to 7 p.m.) they earn an estimated 80 pesos ($8) which is more than the minimum daily wage for laborers.

I asked what their parents thought about this work and Carlos said that both he and his brother were too young to get hired at the factories. Neither of them wants to beg but they both need to bring home money for the family. He said that this was "respectable" work. His father, he said, was a day laborer and was working right now cleaning up a construction site. His mother was at home. There were four other children ranging in age from four months to seven years. The mother had worked in the past: she had sold holy cards outside the cathedral but was run off twice by the more established vendors and once by the police because she did not have a license.

Felipe is proud of his act. He said that his mother helps him each morning with the makeup and costume. He practices tumbling and juggling at night and hopes to be able to juggle four balls ("or even knives") in the future.

Both made faces when I asked about school. They both felt that they were working men, helping their families. Carlos replied to my questions about education by saying that, if someone were foolish enough to insist that they go to school, there would be much less food on the table and (pointedly) no new tennis shoes for his little brother.

LAVAPARABRISAS. (Windshield Washers). Whether it needs washing or not, you may find your windshield covered with soapy water and a youngster stretched across the hood wiping it down. These boys are quick, and the slightest nod or even failure to immediately yell "¡No, gracias!" will be taken as permission to proceed. Once the soapsuds have covered the driver's side of the windshield, you might as well let them finish. Sometimes even when they are finished your visibility will be less than you'd like. You either drive off with opaque streaks obscuring your vision, or ask the boy to catch a spot he missed, risking the ire of the backed-up traffic behind you.

It's no doubt hard to do a good job of washing a windshield in the middle of heavy traffic with only seconds to complete the task. And then there's the problem of obtaining refills of clean water for the bucket. So for a one-peso coin (10 cents), it's no big deal to let the boy take a crack at it. Sometimes you get lucky and it is cleaned almost as well as you could do it yourself. And even the most reluctant customer is forced to admire the energy, the initiative and good-natured enthusiasm of these workers. None are over fifteen, most considerably younger. They are out there working in the hot sun, dangerously leaping in and out of traffic, breathing in the fumes of several thousand cars each day, yet always with a smile, a quip, a polite *"Muchas gracias. ¡Que le vaya bien!"* for the customer before he drives off.

LOS CANTANTES. (The Singers). Whether riding the electric bus (*par vial*) or the exhaust-spewing jitneys, the trip across town is occasionally made more pleasant by the appearance of a guitar-toting minstrel. Usually it is an elderly man dressed in Levis, cowboy hat, western shirt and boots. He climbs aboard the bus, without being charged a fare by the driver, and then braces himself in a standing position a few feet in front of the fare box. There he will sing two or three traditional ballads before departing through the rear door. On his way out he will pass among the passengers for tips. Seldom does his act last more than ten or fifteen minutes.

Most of the singers I've encountered were fairly competent guitarists. Their playing of that instrument was even more of a tour de force because of the rocking of the old buses, the sudden stops and turns, the standing-room-only crowds. And I have never seen one of these balladeers take a seat. They always stand *muy firme* with legs spread, and maintain a precarious balance on the wildly rocking buses without missing a note and without the support of the overhead bar.

The voices of these singers generally range from indifferent to bad. But, considering the fact that some of them seem to be in their seventies or eighties, one is inclined to make allowances. Actually, their singing is not hard to take. Most are usually better than George Burns, but with the same kind of geriatric charm.

Occasionally one is pleasantly surprised by the quality of these performances. Once on my way downtown an old man with a guitar brought his ten-year-old grandson aboard the bus. They were both dressed in worn but presentable charro outfits. The child sang the quatrains of the ballad while his grandfather accompanied him on the guitar. The child's voice was extraordinary. It was a purissimo falsetto, true-pitched and tonally perfect. It was the kind of voice one might have heard in St. Peter's at Rome in the days of Pope Gregory. A voice that pierced the heart with its beauty.

In addition to the standard ballads, some of the old men sing *corridos* or narrative poems set to music which recount a historical event or a village story of tragedy. Sometimes these will be mini-histories on the life and time of Emiliano Zapata, Pancho Villa, Francisco Madero or other heroes of the Revolution. Others may be poems of love and tragic passion, betrayal, family drama, or simply *la vida dura* (Mexican blues).

I was riding buses for about three months before I was fortunate enough to hear one of these serenades. I found it delightful. I also determined that the best buses for encountering these musicians were the ones either going to or coming from El Centro. In the upscale neighborhoods and the outlying sections performers of any kind are rare.

Besides these minstrels, once occasionally encounters someone singing a hymn a cappella and selling religious tracts or holy pictures afterward. Once on a bus to San Miguel Allende there was a poet who recited some of his work and then sold photocopies of his works at the end.

The a cappella singer I heard had more spirit than talent. And the poet? Well, his recitation was a bit too rapid for me to be a fair judge but his energy was akin to Ginsberg's reading of "Howl" at City Lights Bookstore in San Francisco back in the Fifties. Later I treated him to a Coke and we talked about Octavio Paz's *Dias Habiles* (which he was then reading) and *Piedra del Sol* which I had recently read. He was a young man with high hopes for the transcendental possibilities of poetry. When we parted I wished him well and copied down a few lines he had quoted from a poem of Paz's. I still carry in my wallet the scrap of paper on which it wrote them. *¡Que extraño saberse vivo!/Caminar entre la gente/con el secreto a voces de estar vivo.* "How strange to know yourself as alive!/To walk among people/with the open secret of being alive."

TRAGAFUEGOS. (Fire Eaters). On those rare occasions when it is not recalcitrant from the cheap gas I put into it because of the shortages of Magna Sin (unleaded), I drive my 1978 Mercury around the city. Yesterday, while stopped at the traffic light on the corner of Justo Sierra and López Mateos, I came upon a practitioner of what is without doubt the most dangerous of the street professions: fire eating. The performer doesn't actually eat fire as did Brutus's wife, but what he does do is equally dangerous and ultimately as fatal.

This corner also occasionally features a Huichol Indian dressed in full regalia. He has a colorful headdress, a painted face, and gourd rattles attached to his ankles. He pounds incessantly on a small drum and plays a flute which apparently is capable of only three notes. The resultant cacophony is both alien and sad. He is a native in this part of Mexico and yet it appears as if he's in another country populated by foreigners who find him strange. I've never seen anyone give him money. Nor have I seen him ask for any. He just plays the interminable drum, toots the interminable flute, up one side of the street and down the other. He'll disappear for weeks at a time and then return.

But today the drum-beating, flute-playing Huichol is elsewhere. Today, as I sit in traffic waiting for the light to change, a young man in his early twenties fills his mouth with diesel fuel from a plastic jug. He lights a makeshift torch (a rag wrapped around a wire coat hanger), and then strides confidently towards the three lanes of stopped traffic. He stares at the drivers. Then, leaning back, he spits the combustible liquid towards the flame of the outstretched torch. A burst of flame spews forth from his mouth and travels a good fifteen feet into traffic. The heat from the fire can be felt three cars back from where he is standing. It is so strong that it singes the hairs on my forearm leaning out the open window.

Fire eaters earn more than any of the other street performers. However, their colorful careers are often cut short. Several studies have been done on the effects of corrosive petroleum fluids on the mouth, stomach and brains of these "artists." Experts at the Autonomous University of Mexico list the following as progressive steps in the Fire Eater Syndrome: (1) Loss of sense of taste; (2) Gum inflammation; (3) Loss of feeling in the mouth; (4) Ulcers of the mucous lining next to the tongue, (5) Irreversible brain damage; (6) Death. The progression from 1 to 6 takes usually no more than two years.

I park the car in the bank lot across the street and take a few notes on this young man in the next-to-last-category of street performer. Literally a dying breed. He is fairly cocky; a bit like a prize fighter. After he finishes his performance, he struts up to each car and collects a handful of coins. He walks like a man who knows that he is killing himself to amuse others and who deserves whatever (excuse the pun) the traffic will bear. When he takes a break I go over to talk with him.

The gasoline odor is overpowering. He has a large plastic jug of it at his side, along with several rags for torches, and a plastic container of

Kool Aid. There are several fresh facial burns on his cheeks, his nose, his ears. His eyebrows are singed. His hair is covered by a water-soaked red bandanna. There is an odor about him of burnt flesh and hair which is nauseating. This will be a short interview.

Perhaps shorter than I thought... He at first mistakes me for a policeman, then for a government health worker. I tell him that I'm a writer and he suspiciously asks: "Then, where is your camera?" He assumes that any legitimate writer would want a picture of him performing his act. He thinks that this is the most interesting thing about himself, and can't imagine that words alone could cover the drama of it.

His speech is slurred and he has a hard time sorting out his words. We have some difficulty with the facts. He tells me, for instance, that he is nineteen on one occasion, and twenty-three on another. He tells me that he used to be a book salesman and that he went to primary school. Later he tells me that he was studying to be a lawyer! Hardly a credible narrator. After some more discussion he claims that on a good day he can average about $20, which is the salary of a grammar school teacher here. I ask him how much he's made today and he shows me his money can. It looks to be about $8 worth of pesos and he has been working less than two hours.

Several years ago in Mexico City officials rounded up all these fire eaters and took them to detox clinics. They treated them medically, gave them some job training, and then put them back out on the streets. Most of the jobs they trained them for did not exist, however, and "created" jobs (such as selling paperback copies of the classics on street corners on commission) were so ill-rewarded that most of them returned to their old profession.

TRANSITOS. (Traffic Police). Here in Guadalajara the *transitos* will usually run the fire eaters off if they see them. However, I'm told that it's possible to get the *transitos* to look the other way for a modest sum.

Also, if one knows which corner and at what time the *transito* will be on duty, one can choose another corner and another time to ply one's trade.

At the height of the tourist season there will often be four or five *transitos* at an intersection directing traffic. Usually this will be an intersection which has a perfectly functioning automatic traffic light. It appears they often place themselves in areas where their blue and white uniforms can be seen to advantage. They will flash their white gloves in inexplicable signs, blow whistles, run in and out of traffic—as if to say: "No need to worry. You see we have everything under control!"

However, if sometimes they seem superfluous in some areas, in other parts of town (detours, construction sites, non-functioning traffic lights) they are conspicuous by their absence.

Transitos take themselves very seriously. The average citizen, however, is less than impressed and accords them a minimum of respect. Of all the street "performers" (with the possible exception of the Chiclet sellers), the *transitos* probably have the least status and are the lowest paid for actual hours of work. That they might be tempted to supplement their income by threatening to confiscate your license for a traffic violation is entirely understandable. The $5 "donated" to hold on to your licence is generally a bargain. A trip to traffic court with its interminable wait would likely cost you a day's pay plus a fine. Almost never is the defendant found *not* guilty.

It is impossible to drive in Mexico without committing a half dozen traffic violations during the course of an average day. Traffic lights often do not function during the rainy season. Even when they do, cars will commonly run them. Often, sections of roadbeds are washed out. Chassis-jarring potholes prohibit drivers from staying in their proper lanes with any consistency. Also, the ubiquitous *glorietas* (traffic circles) have no hard-and-fast lane rules. Even if they did, they'd be unenforceable.

Driving in Mexico requires a Zen-like sense of flow and an acceptance of anarchy which, once accommodated, can actually make the experience, if not pleasant, at least stimulating. On the positive side, Mexicans rarely use horns. They flash their lights when annoyed and when preparing to pass. They rarely yell and almost never get physically aggressive.

While I have no statistical evidence to support my thesis, I'm inclined to think that driving in Mexico is probably safer than north of the border. In the ten years I've been driving here I've witnessed fewer accidents and found a higher level of courtesy and serenity than driving in equally populated urban areas in the United States.

The *transitos* I've met have been invariably helpful and courteous. And the drivers (though themselves erratic) have been tolerant of my wrong moves. I've never had a Mexican flip me the bird (a daily occurrence in Boston), or yell at me out the window. The police are certainly less intrusive here. As a newcomer to Denver, Colorado, twenty years ago, I garnered three moving violations in a week for a total of nine points off my license and $350 in fines. Any one of them: going the wrong way on a one way street, making a right turn on a red light, and making an unauthorized U-turn would have been winked at in Mexico or would have garnered no more than a warning. The system here is a bit looser but, in my observation, no more hazardous than more stringently policed communities.

So… these are the street people of Mexico. A colorful lot and mostly hard-working. They are generally good-natured and they are unfailingly polite. They exhibit the essential characteristics of most Mexicans: family solidarity, shared spiritual values, willingness to work, and innate courtesy. There is a solid inner core of serenity among them even in the midst of day-to-day stresses. Their contribution to the ambience of Guadalajara makes it unlike any other city of comparable size north of the border. Too bad it is not an exportable commodity.

RATTUS, RATTUS, ET AL.

Rattus rattus, et al. can scale a brick wall two hundred feet high like the one "big as a beaver on his hind legs," who greeted (she said), the New York society matron in her penthouse high above the East River still wet from its evening swim. Also known as the roof rat.

Your lover mumbled, "Seagulls!" as they scuttled across the Sag Harbor shingles in the late night and you listened in sleepless reverie. Now you know. The roof rat *eats* seagulls, leaves no evidence. Hungry enough he'll devour bone, feathers, excrement.

Rattus rattus, also known as the house rat, can climb the inside of a sewer, a drain hole, a water pipe, does not drown easily, can move comfortably up a one and a half inch tube. Whoosh! As much fun as a water slide, coming down the drain, slithering up the sewer pipe of the Union Square Hotel. He's in the toilet bowl now. Hear the splash? Go check! Not there? Only the splatter of drops around the bowl. You can't be sure. It could have been yourself, a previous guest, the maid, who dripped those few discreet drops. Surely not the black rat who can jump two feet straight up, be at your throat as you bend to brush your teeth, then broadjump four feet, gone before you've turned your head: like that! squeezed through a hole the size of a quarter.

Rattus rattus, et al. (especially New World cousin *Neotoma cinera*, old wood rat) enjoy old stucco houses in the West; they make good nests. They like corn and tortillas, also warm milk and will gnaw the nipples off a sleeping cow, devour the white moustache of a suckling pup.

Rattus rattus. Also known as the ship rat. They get on board by climbing hawsers while the vessel is docked at port. They make themselves at home, enjoy the status of stowaways, explore; did not pay a fare and have no loyalty. Thus, *will* desert a sinking ship and cling to bits of flotsam long past the hour the heartiest of men have perished in the cold Atlantic. Ship rats have been found in ocean swells treading water or clinging to wreckage weeks after the ship was lost. And rescuers, searching for human survivors, find rats scurrying up their oars into the lifeboats before they can pull back. No time to think, react! Lifeboats have been found filled with rats and rescuers forced overboard or worse, if empty clothes be evidence.

Rats love mud walls of old missions, cool shade of *arroyos*, hay and grain of stockyards, droppings of barns, corrals. In Arizona and New Mexico as late as 1988 there were four cases of bubonic plague. Confirmed. That same Black Death which decimated Europe, turned brother against brother, mother against child. In Albuquerque and Tucson fleas jumped off dead rats onto human flesh, swelled up lymph glands, turned the skin black. Those cases contained; hidden now in footnotes of medical journals. But at the Center for Communicable Diseases in downtown Denver, epidemiologists agree: four and not four *million* merely a matter of grace, or luck. Not what rats, of course, trust to.

They depend on breeding, propagation. The superiority of genes. Feats of fornication. Litter after litter not slowed by seasons or nine month incubations. Not constrained by condoms or Popes, AIDS, Planned Parenthood. They know the tricks of the white man to decimate their race. They breed with a terrible dedication for survival. They overpopulate, then look for *Lebensraum* any place they can find it.

A rat can gnaw through wood, through mortar, through half inch metal. A rat can gnaw through bone, severing limbs. A rat *must* do these things because from infancy he is constantly teething. Gnawing or not, his incisors grow four to six inches a year. If not ground down they will grow up into his brain, killing him slowly with great pain. Rats in confinement, mostly albinos from Norway (*Rattus norvegicus*), have agonized this way, which is how we know. They do not suffer prisons gracefully. In this, as in other things, they are much like us. Confinement breeds psychotic behavior, overcrowding, violence: vicious attacks on offspring, sodomy on siblings, voracious cannibalism. Very unratlike. Such "dirty rats" are more likely to be found in antiseptic labs on Midwest campuses than in Manhattan sewers.

Rats are omnivorous but prefer grain: oats, wheat, barley—high in fiber, low in cholesterol. Their favorite meal: the complete protein formed by wheat bread and peanut butter. A professional rat killer by the name of Clyde Barstow taught me this and other things when we worked together on a summer job. South of Boston were rats in the cellar of a Roxbury tenement: fatter than rabbits, meaner than alley cats.

We fed them peanut butter sandwiches, Clyde and I, laced with a chemical which ruptured the intestines. They were in terrible agony, projectile vomiting great gobs of black blood. They would jump convulsively at Clyde and me, somehow *knowing* it was we who did it. And, though I stood on the top cellar step with a .22 Ruger and knee-high boots, I trembled till they crawled away to die, someplace I would not follow. I tremble still.

The offspring of a pregnant rat killed this way will be immune to the chemicals which finished her. More wary, meaner. Which is why rat poisons get more baroque each year. Strychnine lately does nothing more to city rats than make them angry, shake their heads, stare at you with red eyes which say: *Big mistake, pig meat!* To them you and the pig are similar: the smell of the flesh, the taste.

Rats bide their time. Where there is no peanut butter, no wheat bread, rats will eat a bird, a lamb, a piglet (see above). They will eat the flesh of infants left alone in cribs: the parent tired of the red-faced brat, crying over nothing night after night, and no longer checking to see. They will also eat adults not strong enough to beat them away, as in a nursing home in Tennessee where one woman lost an ear and then, weakened by age, or terror, or incredulous dismay, did not call out or move away.

In Molokai, not far from beaches where tourists lie in the sun today, is a Catholic leper colony whose patients (extremities numbed by that disease) could not feel the pain when rats sat on their chins and ate the lips away, the nose. Even fingers and toes, so that medical journals reported those parts rotted away from leprosy. Not so. But rats thrive on misinformation and chomped on for months till Father Damien and an observant doctor saw for themselves one quiet night.

Opportunistic, most agree, *Rattus rattus, et al.,* and much maligned. Imaginative, but not unkind. Their main goal to stay alive, adapt (survival of the species and all that). They are quick-brained, adaptable (like us to some degree) which is why scientists study them and learn how many part of carcinogens per thousand it takes till they succumb. Laymen say: *Tush, tush, that's a rat, not I!* But rats survive *cum* smokers lungs, cirrhosis, metastasis, *sans* vital parts. We don't know why. And when one dies, how carefully it conceals its art from probing eyes.

JOURNAL IN A RAINY SEASON

June 10th. It is the second week in June and it has not rained in over six months. Situated on a high plateau, Guadalajara has only two seasons: *la temporada de sequía* and *la temporada de lluvias*. We are approaching, everyone devoutly hopes, the end of the dry season. The air tastes of dust, bleached bones, and one perspires after walking only two blocks.

The corn has been in the ground for almost a month and, though it is a special drought-resistant hybrid, it will die soon if there is no moisture. Most of it is planted on land where there is no irrigation, no hope of water without the rains. The temperature is in the nineties and since May it has been torturously uncomfortable working at our school. The children are restless and distracted. There is no air conditioning; there are no coolers or fans. When I write on the blackboard my hand leaves a wet half moon beneath each word.

June 14th. At 3 p.m. the sky begins to darken. Dark gray storm clouds move in from the mountains; blue-gray thunderheads begin forming and the horizons fold inward. The birds begin to chatter and hole up in the eucalyptus and jacaranda along the tree-lined avenues. Traffic speeds up on López Mateos; people are nervous, hurrying to outrace the storm.

A wind picks up the scraps of papers and trash from the gutters and vacant lots; dust blows into our eyes. It is a dry wind yet, and could presage nothing more than a dust storm. It's happened before with the rain clouds moving south to Mexico City and passing us by. But by this time I think it is the real thing. The mongrel dogs, who slink around the taco stand hoping for scraps, have already sought shelter under the trees. Trusting their instincts, we quicken our pace, headed home *sans* umbrella and raincoats but with our precious grade books and lesson plans sensibly covered in plastic. As long as they're protected (ten months work) nothing too terrible can befall us.

The heat is still oppressive, except that now it is muggy as well. Then, as we turn the corner onto Justo Sierra, great drops of rain begin falling. Globules of rain. I am reminded of the old Irish priest in my childhood parish splattering holy water. The drops feel like the first blessing on Easter Sunday if one sits in the front pew: large, cool, miraculous, this newly blessed water from a golden device striking one's head with the shock of a second baptism. The rain falls like that, in enormous, discrete drops, cold and pure.

Before we can reach our house, the whole sky opens up and the drops are replaced by sheets of rain borne by the wind, now east, now west, north then south, so that by the time we enter our courtyard and unlock the door, there is not a centimeter of our clothing left unsoaked. The temperature has dropped thirty degrees Fahrenheit in less than twenty minutes. In our wet clothes we are not merely cool, we are shivering.

The wind blows the curtains of our living room in with great powerful sweeps. Student essays are scattered from the desk, a lamp falls to the floor. Lightning flashes in the distance, thunder rumbles like flapping sheet metal, or the sound of lumber trucks crossing a distant bridge.

Now the windows rattle and crack as if they're about to break, as if rocks were being thrown against them. We open the door and see hailstones the size of mothballs bouncing and pinging off the tile in the entryway. Several bounce into our living room. I pick one up. It is opaque, milky-white, not delicate like a snowflake or crystaline like ice. It has a musty odor and does not melt quickly in my hand. I forego the temptation to taste it. It has come a long way through a dusty and polluted atmosphere and can do me no good. Besides it *looks* poisonous. And why doesn't it melt?

Now the hail surrenders to the rain which no longer falls in wind-whipped sheets but pours, buckets, cascades down, as if the sky had opened up and emptied itself of the accumulated rain of generations. It is clearly a monsoon rain such as occur in the Orient or (for a few days in late August) in the Sonoran Desert of Arizona. In Central Mexico these storms are called *tormentas* and, as time goes by in this rainy season, we will discover the aptness of that word.

So much water has come out of the sky one would think the whole city would be inundated. (That's actually happened quite often in the past. Cars floating in streets that had become rivers; *arroyos* turned into brown water rapids and cataracts which swept away everything in their path: cattle, dogs, Huicholes caught unawares.) But then, as suddenly as it began, as if a giant hand had simply turned off a celestial faucet, the rain ceases.

The sun returns, steam rises from the streets, there is the sound of church bells close by and sirens in the distance. Large Sinaloan crows splash in the pools. The giant eucalyptus trees drip and fill the air with their pungency. Electric green hummingbirds (and violet-throated ones!) appear from nowhere to drink the sweetness of hibiscus and jasmine. Doves coo steadily, rhythmically. The earth smells sweet and rich: the senses are overwhelmed. Somewhere a cock crows, his instincts awry, convinced it is dawn; maybe even something more. Maybe a new earth in a new world.

July 8th. "O, western wind, when wilt thou blow/that the small rain down may rain?" It has been raining virtually non-stop for nine consecutive days. The radio says that six *colonias* in Guadalajara are inundated, streets impassable, houses flooded. In other parts of the country the newspapers report twenty people dead and more than 7,000 homeless. The Agricultural Secretariat announced today that forty percent of the corn and wheat crops were ruined in the states of Morelos, Puebla, Oaxaca and Hidalgo. In Matamoros heavy rains closed four major highways and several bridges gave way.

Earlier, friends of ours going to the U.S. said that the only real highway to the States from Guadalajara was closed after a two kilometer section of the pass through the *barrancas* collapsed. That's not the way the rainy season is supposed to work. All the guide books and even Jackson and Rubio's *Standard Spanish Grammar* (for godsakes!) plainly state that, during the rainy season, Mexico stays sunny for most of the day. The skies are clear until late afternoon when the storm clouds move in. Then, usually close enough to four o'clock that you could set your watch by it, thunderheads burst and the well-known *tormenta* with its high winds, lightning, and torrential downpour seizes the day. It lasts about an hour. Then the skies clear up, the sun appears in all its south-of-the-border benevolence; dancing rainbows light the horizon, the birds sing. It is beautiful. All the books say that. People who have lived here for years add that the rain is a welcome treat, generally; kind of a pleasant cooling off in the late afternoon followed by a leisurely walking under the trees or drinking margaritas at a sidewalk cafe.

It is not that way this year. It is cold, damp and, while the rains slacken from time to time, they never completely cease. Our Mexican friends tell us that this is very unusual. Unique to their experience, in fact. It has never rained like this before. The weather reports on t.v. (on those evenings when there is electrical power) say that it is a freak Caribbean storm. The meteorological satellite maps show heavy cloud formations settled comfortably over 85% of the country.

This is bad news for the millions of people who have booked expensive hotel rooms (there are no cheap ones) in the path of the solar eclipse which will soon arrive at Baja California Sur, cross the mainland at Nayarit, then move on to Guadalajara. Rooms are sold out at all hotels for this entire week at three times the going rate. This is the astronomical event of the era. It will not occur again in this part of the world until April 8, 2024. The next total eclipse in North American won't be until August 21, 2017. And now the weatherman says that the entire area is overcast with no likelihood of change projected. The ironies of nature. Doesn't God know we're all going to be watching? Is this some kind of celestial joke?

We had chosen Mexico as a place to live and work rather than other equally beautiful and fascinating places—such as Seattle or Costa Rica—because such stretches of rain and damp were unheard of here. Both Lucinda and I thrive on sunshine and the quality of light which exists in Southern California and the Southwest United States and Mexico. Three days of rain makes us feel like caged animals: restless, ill at ease, avoiding conflict, carefully choosing our words lest we end up spitting and snarling at each other like two cats drowning in a sack.

After four days our nerves are worn from dampness, power outages, the darkness, the steady rain. Misunderstood remarks, a small difference of opinion, a subtle change in the inflection of voice can send either of us into a stomach-knotting rage. The salt shaker clogs even with the precautionary rice grains. The front door is warped from moisture and rattles like a rusty bear trap when it finally opens.

After six days of rain we do not talk at all except for one to ask the other for a cup of tea. She is in her sewing room now working on a quilt. I already know that her carefully selected cloth, now dampened by the weather, no longer feels right to her. I know that it bunches in unacceptable ways, that the stitches pull at inappropriate places. I know that she is gradually building up a self-punishing exasperation about her work which will make her companionship even more problematical as the day wears on.

As for myself, I had wanted to write a fairly upbeat short story today. It was to be about my father sitting in his old Plymouth listening to the last innings of a Red Sox game on his car radio. The year was 1958. Eisenhower was President and his staff drove the new Edsel. Ted Williams was thinking about retirement. The story was to be nostalgic and mildly humorous. But the first draft of the story made me miserable. Not only did it not "work," but I found myself examining all the neurotic behaviors of my family which forced my father out of the house in the first place to seek solace from a car radio in the rain. Yeah, the rain again. I can't get away from it.

There's a hole in my psyche where a black rain pours through. I go into the bathroom and take a hot shower. When I get out, the towels are damp and cold. I dry myself off as best I can and then return to my desk. Dissatisfaction lays heavily on everything I do. The word processor won't print clearly because the paper is damp. I am writing now with a blue Bic pen which does fine until it comes to a random damp spot on the legal pad and then I have to write the same word (word) twice (twice).

July 9th. This is the tenth day of incessant rain. I am writing now only to cure spiritual uneasiness. My generous-spirited nature is being swept away like the bougainvillaea vines torn from the patio walls by the deluge. Throughout the building there are sounds of incessant squabbling, family arguments. In our apartment there is the heavy silence from fear of quarreling which wears me down. I write to push away the loneliness which leers in the darkened window of my study. It is a presence-in-an-absence, a weight on my chest which tells me that I need *something!* a drink, a cigarette, a blood transfusion. Dismal. Dank. *Las tormentas.*

In *A Farewell To Arms* Hemingway has Catherine say about the rain: "Sometimes I see myself dead out there." I don't feel that way exactly but I can empathize with the emotion (or lack of emotion) which would bring a character to say that, or an author to write it. It is not just psychological. Or spiritual. There is a definite physical pull to this kind of weather. The body becomes heavier. The lungs fill with fluid. Sounds seem to reach the ear from a much greater distance. One lives in artificial light. My stomach feels like there is something growing in it. No amoebas, although they are fairly commonplace here, but something even more malignant, like a cancerous yeast, or worse. More like the kind of gray parasitic fungi which grow on damp trees in rain forests. I feel bloated, despite the fact that all I've had to eat all day was a bowl of soup and a couple of tortillas.

The children in the apartment above us have been playing *Lotería Nacional,* their own imitation of the national lottery drawing which is held each week in Mexico City. It consists of young boys dressed in colorful pageboy livery (each looking for all the world like a clone of the "Call For Philip Morris" midget) screaming the lottery winners out to a live (but presumably deaf) audience. The kids upstairs are calling out: *"CUARENTA Y CINCO , ONCE. ¡VIENTE MILLONES DE PE- SOS! CATORCE, VIENTICINCO. ¡DIEZ MILLONES DE PESOS!"* They have been doing it for the past fifteen minutes, not even pausing for a breath.

It never ceases to amaze me how much tolerance Mexican parents have for this kind of thing. A North American parent would long ago have screamed at these kids to SHUT UP! or would have resorted to physical violence by this point. But I can imagine the Mexican father looking over at his wife, catching her eye and smiling. Maybe he even says, "These little rascals. What will they think of next?" These parents must be doing something right though. The students I teach here in Mexico are the best adjusted group of kids I've taught anywhere: self-confident but courteous, cooperative but independent. At the American School in Guadalajara a major disciplinary problem is someone smoking in the boy's rest room. No drugs, no violence, no disrespect to teachers. Mexican youth are their nation's best advertisement.

But there's a powerful downpour now which rattles the windows, slashes across the few strands of ivy still left clinging to the back wall, and timpanis off the drains. It effectively drowns out the voices of the children. I am saved the unpleasant duty of banging on their door to tell the parents (politely) that, while I appreciate the long-term results of Mexican child-rearing tactics, their methods today are imperiling my sanity.

My life seems drawn out today, tentative, without passion or energy. It is a pinched, crab-like existence. Rain or no rain I am going for a walk. Maybe I can come back revived, with more oxygen in my blood, my brain. Maybe even the hope of becoming absorbed in a new way of seeing, which will jump off the page, electric, vital; the words I wished I could write but was too depressed by the weather to manage.

I am slightly disappointed (reading over my notes) that what has cost me so much depression and strain for the past ten days could be summed up in words of so low an emotional content. The silver tongue has become tarnished in the dampness. Or perhaps, it was not sterling to begin with, only silverplate. Still, I will keep my sense of proportion, my balance, even if that amounts to nothing more than purging myself of the obsession that I can be better than I am.

GREEN, I LOVE YOU, GREEN

Under the greenwood tree I write this paean to the color of youth, and hope, and freedom. Wearing clothing of green was prohibited in Ireland under the British Penal Laws because it was the color of Irish revolt. "For they're hanging men and women," the Celtic poet wrote, "for wearing of the green." My mother told me, with pride, the lovely defiance of having an Irish son with clear green eyes.

Green has always been the color of revolution and hope. In the green of July when the apples were new, the French shouted, "*Liberté, Egalité, Fraternité*," under a green banner, months before the *tricolore* was their flag.

In New York, Central Park forms a greenbelt in the city. In New Hampshire, the Green Mountains form the northern end of the Appalachians. The Green Mountain Men fought in the Revolution. Vermont itself, derived its name from the French *vert*, itself green, or verdure, and the Spanish *verde*, as in Lorca's "*Verde que te quiero verde.* Green, I love thee green."

Green is positive. To Whitman, the grass is like our lives, "out of hopeful green stuff woven." We've been given the green light on the project, the okay, the go-ahead. We're trusted, permitted, allowed. It's also an open place where folks can speak their mind, as in "The protesters organized on the village green." In the South they eat greens, usually cooked with pork. They are collard or mustard greens. If you ask for greens in England, however, you'll be given cabbage. Another reason for a revolution if you ask me. You didn't ask? Well, here's another point. In golf if you're close to the green, you've done well. You're in good shape, close to the hole. Actually the whole damn thing is called the green, but the greenest part, the "green" is even fairer than the "fairway".

If a soldier is green it means he's inexperienced, which is not a compliment. The "green-eyed monster" of Shakespeare is jealousy. For Greeks, whose complexions are more olive, "Green with fear," a Homeric term, means pale. Green sand is perfect for founding metal, and green meat could either be freshly killed or in an advanced state of decay. Green sickness is a type of iron deficiency anemia which affects only adolescent girls. It is also called chlorosis and is not fatal. Iron pills seem to do the trick.

The green room is where the talk show guests must wait when they're not required on stage. A greenhouse is not green at all but usually made of glass and heated so that plants can grow in the cold weather, or flowers be forced to bloom.

William Blake claimed England was "a green and pleasant land." But the Irish poet preferred the "green banks of Shannon." A tune "Green grow the lilacs O" sung by Yankee soldiers in Mexico is thought to have given rise to the name *gringo* which has stuck. In Wales, poet Dylan Thomas wrote: "Time held me green and golden, though I sang in my chains like the sea." The sea is often green. Pastures, too, and parrots, leaves and grass, most trees in summer, and evergreens all the time, hence their name. "Greensleeves" was the first song written in English—at least six hundred years before Shakespeare had his actors sing "Under the greenwood tree" in *As You Like It*.

Lady MacBeth was afraid that MacDuff's murder had put so much blood on her hands that it would incarnadine the sea "making the green one red." Greenstick fractures are the worst kind, the bone is partly broken and partly bent. Enough to make you green around the gills. If you are at this point, you might go to the bathroom. If you were in Saudi Arabia, you might find some green soap which is made from potassium hydroxide and linseed oil. Very good for the skin, they tell me.

Back already? Well, let me tell you about greenstone. Not jade, although it, too, is a green stone. No, this one is basalt rock which is altered by cholite or epidote. Not so valuable as jade, but pretty. Green corn is sweet and makes the very best tamales. Ask anyone who lives in Sonora. You could also ask a greengrocer but that's an English produce man and he probably wouldn't know much about Mexican corn.

Speaking of immigrants, they're usually called greenhorns because they are new to the country or the language. Someone green to the job or the task is called that, too. A greenheart, however, is a tropical hard-wood found in South America. The jungles of South America, by the way, have green parrots but no green monkeys. The latter are found only in West Africa, with their green-gray backs. Mexico has green *chiles* which are *muy picantes*. Green peppers, however, are the sweet kind, also called bell peppers which are quite mild.

Green manure is not manure at all but a nitrogen-fixing plant like clover which is plowed under for fertilizer. In some countries, however, it is real manure which has not yet decomposed. A smelly business (Careful where you step!), which is as good a reason as any to go to the Green River which flows from Wyoming into Utah, after which it is not green at all but brown from bottomlands and spills until it empties into the Colorado which in Spanish means red-colored, which it is not, although the cliffs above it are. You might, however, see a green heron on this river, which is a small bird with glossy green wings.

Gangrene has nothing at all to do with green except the way it sounds. It's from the Greek work for dripping sore. Greenbacks refer to U.S. currency which originally were printed only on the back to save money. In 1874 the Greenback Party urged that they be issued to replace all existing currency including gold and silver. That's enough to make you see green. The color of green in certain places does not refer to nature at all, but unhappily to the color of money. But that says more about them than us, right?

The green dragon is not a dragon either but an American arenaceous herb. Green Bay is a city in Wisconsin, home of the Green Bay Packers, which was a team that earned its backers greenbacks back when the Packers had backs.

Greenwich Time is the standard for the world and Greenwich, Connecticut, has one of the largest per capita incomes. Greenville, Mississippi, however, has one of the lowest. There's a university in Greensboro, North Carolina, and a nice college in Greenville, South Carolina. Greenock, however, is a quiet seaport town in Scotland with only a village school.

The green-winged teal is a beautiful fresh water duck found in Europe and America. The greenlet is a vireo, a small bird which is sometimes called the greenfinch. Greening means to restore a forest, and a greenhead is a male mallard.

"We have done but greenly," Shakespeare says, meaning we have just made a beginning. But I'm getting tired, are you? A few more? Okay. Did you know that when the wheat is green in Nebraska it is not green at all but a golden color and ready to cut? Or that green around the gills (mentioned earlier and now a reality!) is a metaphor derived from a greenling which is a fresh water fish found among algae and rocks in the North Atlantic which actually has green gills?

Speaking of the North Atlantic and cold places, let's look at Greenland. Greenland is the largest island in the world (if you don't count Australia which is actually considered a continent). Greenland is in North America but is owned by Denmark. Denmark in North America, are you sure? Yeah, I checked it twice. I don't know what happened.

Maybe the Monroe Doctrine only applies in temperate climes.

Greenshank is a common shorebird—it's also European, as is the common green finch, and the greengage plum. Greenery, however, and green algae are world-wide and live *sin fronteras*. The green gland, too, is found in decapod crustaceans which circle the globe—crabs, lobsters, prawns and shrimp. Greenheads, too, or male mallards, don't seem to be nationalistic.

Actually "life springs forever green," as Goethe once wrote, and "children are heard on the green," in Blake's *Songs of Innocence*. "The force that through the green fuse drives the flower/Drives my green life," wrote Dylan Thomas. And in the *Book of Common Prayer* we read: "He bringest forth... green herbs for the service of men." In Ireland, wrote Dermot Healy, "green cannot be defined as a color only, but as a state of being that follows on the heels of a summer rain."

So, as Pound said; "Pull down vanity I say pull it down!/Learn of the green world." Enjoy life in the green of your youth for it is written in Scripture: "In the morning it is green and groweth up, but in the evening it is dry and withered. Or, in the words of Seamus Heaney, "Green and heavy headed/weighted down by huge sods."

I know, I know, in Greenwich Village you could find a better ending but I'm a green hand at this kind of essay.

And now they're trying, all who can
To shoot the sleepy greencoat man.

THE CONFEDERATE AIR FORCE
COMES TO GUADALAJARA

Soldiers line the tarmac. Automatic weapons with toy-like plastic stocks, but real bullets, are borne by boys with coal-black eyes. They flirt with *las muchachas.* The girls are excited by the fiesta mood of the crowd, the boys' eyes drawn to their short skirts, to a naked shoulder slipping from a blouse.

It is the last week of the rainy season. Already *La Zapopanita*, tiny Virgin of corn paste, has been carried to the Basilica. We are safe from plague for another year; protected from the rains which flood the *arroyos*, wash away the crops, uproot the ancient trees.

The vintage planes rev their engines. The loud speaker plays Glenn Miller. My good friend sways to the old familiar tunes. Nostalgia and excitement merge in him like the confluence of two rugged rivers.

The loudspeaker announces *el piloto* of the first plane will be *CAPITAN JEE-MEE O'BREE-HAN OF TAY-HAHS.* O'Brian of Texas. The Irish, as mother says, are everywhere. Here, too, they are loved. For in Mexico, when *los Yanquis* said: War! the Irish deserted in droves, fought along side their fellow Catholics, and those not killed in battle were hanged from the gallows in San Angel by the conquering gringos. *Los San Patricios*, those of Saint Patrick, are still green in the Mexican memory, connected to the roots of the ash trees, flying in the green branches.

Now O'Brian of *Tejas* has returned with the entire Confederate Air Force! There is his ghost plane taking off now in the east, his jaunty thumbs-up to the five thousand Mexicans thronging the runway as the soldiers yell at the crowd (rifles at port arms) : *"¡Detrás, detrás, quince metros!"* But the crowd ignores the boy soldiers, pushing forward against the barrels of automatic weapons. The loud speaker is now playing "Danny Boy," and above the lugubrious tune is the sound of the gallant engine in a flimsy metal craft which inspires the crows to wheel from the trees in formation, quiet and disciplined. Something about the day, the air, the music, which makes the crowd forget *Tejas*, (O Hated Republic! O Arrogant State) and think instead of *Capitán O'Breehan, el irlandés*, doing a loop now over the crowd, then another, now climbing up in the morning's perilous sun, and then descending, Flying Tiger teeth on the fuselage, machine gun blazing at an unseen enemy.

This *irlandés* is for us all. And we know him. Just as the *zopilotes* know, blackly secure in their haven of majestic ash trees beyond the furrowed fields in the darkening morning with the old corn stalks drying. Just as the hawks know, banking lazily over the sun flowers, the dandelions, then swooping down through the flame trees to where *un ratón* discovers the world no longer safe.

A bomber takes off now, shining silver and terrible on the dark runway. *"¡MIREN A LA IZQUIERDA!"* the loud speaker blares. The Queen of Terror, *"LA SUPERFORTRESS,"* thundering down the sky. *"TAL VEZ... UNA BOMBA."* And yes! Explosions at the west end of the field: flame, black oily smoke, tremors of the earth!

Thunderheads form over the ash trees: there is rain in the air. The fields grow dark and shadowed. The buzzards crane their bald necks. They know that man is nothing more than a soul holding up a corpse.

But it is this soul, once briefly seen, remembered by old warriors in Legionnaire caps, by my friend singing along (and now dancing!) to

Tommy Dorsey at the end of the rainy season on a damp Mexican airfield, which beckoned us here. There is lightning in the air, the taste of sulphur, and the loud speaker shifting to "Taps" as the fighters fly in formation over the field, the crowd, the soldiers and the young girls, all frozen in place looking upward.

Then one plane peels off from the formation, flies south alone over the hills, in memory of *el piloto perdido*, the one lost, whose soul impregnates the morning sky, who holds us bound together with the furrowed fields, the ash trees, the dying field mouse, young soldiers and old warriors, and the rain coming down in great drops, like holy water sprinkling the faithful.

THE SOLDIERS OF SAINT PATRICK

One of the least known stories of the Irish who came to America in the 1840s is that of the Irish Battalion which fought on the Mexican side in the U.S.-Mexico War of 1846-48. They came to Mexico and died, some gloriously in combat, others ignominiously on the gallows. United under a green banner they participated in all the major battles of the War and were cited for bravery by General López de Santa Anna, the Mexican Commander in Chief and President. At the penultimate battle of the war these Irishmen fought until their ammunition was exhausted and even then tore down the white flag which was raised by their Mexican comrades in arms, preferring to struggle on with bayonets until finally overwhelmed by the Yankees. Despite their brave resistance, however, eighty-five of the Irish battalion were captured and sentenced to bizarre tortures and deaths at the hands of the Americans, resulting in what is even today considered the "largest hanging affair in North America."

THE WAR BEGINS
In the spring of 1846, the United States was poised to invade Mexico, its neighbor to the south. The ostensible reason was to collect on past due loans and indemnities. The real reason was to provide the U.S. with control of the ports of San Francisco and San Diego, the trade route through New Mexico Territory, and the rich mineral resources of

the Nevada Territory—all of which at that time belonged to the Republic of Mexico. The United States had previously offered $5 million to purchase New Mexico Territory and $25 million for California, but Mexico had refused.

U.S. President James K. Polk ordered General Zachary Taylor to take a position south of the Nueces River in Texas with a force of 4,000 men. By January, 1846, the general had built a fort in what was Mexican, or at least disputed, territory on the northern banks of the Rio Grande in an effort to put pressure on the Mexicans to agree to a settlement. Notes the historian Bernard DeVoto: "Polk's intention was clear. This was a show of force intended to give the Mexicans a sense of reality in the settlement of various matters he intended to take up, among them the purchase of California." On April 26, 1846, a Mexican cavalry troop crossed the Rio Grande upstream of Taylor's army. A patrol sent by Taylor to intercept them was attacked and, in the skirmish, eleven Americans were killed and five wounded. When Polk received word of the attack he delivered his war message declaring that since the Mexicans had "shed American blood on American soil" a state of war existed between the United States and Mexico."

Prior to the declaration of war by the U.S., a group of Irish Catholics headed by a crack artilleryman named John Riley deserted from the American forces and joined the Mexicans. Born in Clifden, County Galway, Riley was an expert on artillery and it was widely believed that he had served in the British Army as an officer or a non-com while in Canada prior to enlisting in the American Army. Riley's expertise was to turn this new unit into a crack artillery arm of the Mexican defense. Riley is credited with changing the name of the group from the Legion of Foreigners, and with designing their distinctive flag. Within a year, the ranks of Riley's men would be swelled by Catholic foreign residents in Mexico City, and Irish and German Catholics who deserted once the war broke out, into a battalion known as *Los San Patricios* or "Those of San Patrick."

The San Patricios fought under a green silk flag emblazoned with the Mexican coat of arms, an image of St. Patrick, and the words "Erin Go Braugh" (sic). The battalion was one of artillery and was observed in key positions during every major battle. Their aid was critical because the Mexicans had poor cannon with a range of 400 meters less than the Americans. In addition, Mexican cannoneers were inexperienced and poorly trained. The addition of veteran gunners to the Mexican side would result in at least two major battles being fought to a draw. At the Battle of Buena Vista, for example, the San Patricios held the high ground and enfiladed the Americans. At one point they even wrested cannon from the Yanks, and led General Taylor's advisors to believe that the battle had been lost. Several Irishmen were awarded the Cross of Honor by the Mexican government for their bravery in that battle, and many received field promotions.

At the Battle of Churubusco, holed up in a Catholic monastery and surrounded by a superior force of American cavalry, artillery and infantry, the San Patricios withstood three major assaults and inflicted heavy losses on the Yanks. Eventually, however, a shell struck their stored gunpowder, the ammunition park blew up, and the Irishmen, after a gallant counter-offensive with bayonets, were overwhelmed by sheer numbers. They were tried by a military court-martial, and then scourged, branded and hanged in a manner so brutal that it is still remembered in Mexico today.

In almost every Mexican account of the war, the San Patricios are considered heroes who fought for the noble ideals of religion and a just cause against a Protestant invader of a peaceful nation. In U.S. histories, however, they are often referred to as turncoats, traitors and malcontents who joined the other side for land or money.

REASONS FOR DEFECTION

It seems odd that anyone would defect from a superior force sure of victory, to join an obviously inferior one certain to be defeated. Even if, as most U.S. accounts assert, there were offers of money or land from the Mexicans. There was plenty of free land to the west, much easier to come by than risking one's life in combat against a Yankee army. Simple desertion and seeking refuge in the rich valleys of California would have accomplished that purpose. To determine the true causes of the defection of these men it is necessary to reflect on the temper of the times.

The potato blight which began in 1845 (roughly coinciding with the Mexican War and lasting for its duration) brought devastation to Europe more horrible than the Black Death. For the Irish it was the beginning of massive evictions, starvation, sickness and death. Of the many fortunate enough to afford the fare for an escape to the New World, tens of thousands would die en route as a result of the inhuman conditions aboard Great Britain's vessels.

Victims of oppression in the Old World, they were to experience it again in the New World. Confronted by enormous numbers of Irish-Catholic immigrants in the 1840s, American Nativism raised its ugly head. "All the world knows," wrote historian Thomas Gallagher, "that Yankee hates Paddy." And so it seemed to those who had survived the perilous journey to America only to be labeled inferior by demagogic politicians and feared by Anglo-American workmen.

Victims of prejudice in the New World, it should not be considered strange that they would shortly find themselves becoming sympathetic to the Mexicans. Here was another Catholic people being invaded by Protestant foreigners. According to a contemporary account, "On reaching Mexico they discovered they had been hired by heretics to slaughter brethren of their own church. On top of this they were confronted with the hatred of their fellow soldiers." The intense prejudice of many of the American soldiers, especially the volunteers, has been commented upon by at least one careful historian. According to K. Jack Bauer, author of *The Mexican War:1846-48*, the majority of

American soldiers

> ...were products of a militantly Protestant culture which still viewed Catholicism as a misdirected and misbegotten religion. Although the regulars included a significant number of Catholic enlisted men, the volunteers did not. This strengthened the tendency to ignore the rights and privileges of the church in a Catholic country as well as increase the harassing of that church. Some of the volunteers' acts, like the stabling of horses in the Shrine of San Francisco in Monterrey, so upset the Mexicans that they still mention it in modern works.

ORIGINS OF ANTI-CATHOLICISM IN THE UNITED STATES

America was a nation which was founded by Calvinists who, in rejecting the Church of England, had rejected the hierarchy of both Anglican and Catholic institutions and, in rejecting the spiritual hierarchy, had rejected the temporal one as well. Free to elect their own ministers, they were equally free to elect their own governors. To most Anglo-Saxons living in the United States, this is what it meant to be an American: free of European authority, both that of the Pope and that of the King. Those who still clung to a hierarchical model were considered regressive and unfit for self-government.

The Catholic Church was, to the Calvinist way of thinking, connected politically to a repressive and antiquated system, even more than the Anglican model which they had rejected. Catholics, it was widely believed, had not developed a habit of independent thought. They were still chained to a religion which accepted the Pope, a foreign power, as their authority, rather than their individual consciences. It was believed that not only were Catholics unable to think for themselves in matters of faith or morals, they were equally incapable of being part of a democratic system. Thus, by the early 1800s the Catholic religion was seen at best as retrograde, and—at worst—inimical to a democratic republic.

As early as 1830 the American Bible Society urged the unity of

Protestant sects to combat Rome's influence in the West and expressed the belief that "His Holiness the Pope, has, within his larger grasp, already fixed upon this fair portion of our Union and knows full well how to keep his fold."

While in the early republic there was some tolerance of Catholic minorities, this was to change quickly with the increase in immigration of Irish Catholics during the 1830s and 1840s reaching its crest during the years of the Irish famine, as poor, rural Catholics flooded into the American towns and cities. Anti-Catholic riots broke out in Philadelphia in 1844 and, when they were over, the Irish ghetto lay in ruins, hundreds of homeless Irish roamed the streets, and two Catholic churches were burned to the ground.

Since solidarity in the face of commonly perceived oppression is a universal characteristic of any ethnic or religious group, it is hardly surprising that Irish Catholics would find unity among themselves in the service. As the War progressed and they witnessed more depredations against their co-religionists in Mexico, it is hardly surprising that some Irishmen felt they had more in common with the Mexicans than the invading Americans. The destruction of Catholic churches in Mexico by the invading U.S. Army and other depredations by Protestant volunteers was also been well-documented by both sides. And, just in case they needed a reminder of the connection between the Americans' treatment of the Irish at home and the abuse of Mexicans abroad, Santa Anna's leaflets were widely distributed. They read in part:

> Can you fight by the side of those who put fire to your temples in Boston and Philadelphia? Did you witness such dreadful crimes and sacrileges without making a solemn vow to our Lord? If you are Catholic, the same as we, if you follow the doctrines of Our Savior, why are you murdering your brethren? Why are you antagonistic to those who defend their country and your own God?

Why indeed? Many Irishmen would be quick to see that higher

loyalties should prevail and they would join the Mexican side. They would see that they had more in common with the Mexicans than with the invading army.

THE IRISH "RACE"

The Protestants certainly saw similarities and were quick to point them out. The Mexican they asserted, like the Irishman, was unstable, ignorant, feckless, easily led, and incapable of participation in a republic. Using both the psuedo-science of phrenology and the more respectable science of physiology, contemporary American scientists determined that the short full figures of the Irish indicated that they were "inactive, slothful and lazy." This was a stereotype also applied to the Mexican. The coarse red hair of the Irish showed that they were "excitable and gushing." Their ruddy complexions indicated that they were selfish "with hearty animal passions." Irishmen of this period are variously described as have a "hanging bone gait... the low brow denoting a serf of fifty descents..dark eyes sunken beneath the compressed brows" with a look of "savage ferocity." By the 1840s this legitimization of negative racial characteristics had reached its apex.

MANIFEST DESTINY

Most of those who had settled in America in the 18th and early 19th centuries had no real sense of nationhood. Those in Virginia considered themselves Virginians, those in Texas, Texans or "Texicans," and those from Maine, "Down Easters." Allegiances were territorial rather than nationalistic. When the victorious American Army finally entered Mexico City they played three "national" anthems; *Hail Columbia*, *Yankee Doodle* and the *Star Spangled Banner*. While there was no clear sense of nationhood, Americans were nevertheless in the process of defining who they were. They were doing this essentially by stating quite clearly what an American was **not**. In the 1840s he was not a

Negro, not a Mexican, not an Indian and certainly not Irish Catholic. Notes Dale T. Knobel, Professor of history at Texas A & M:

> ...the Irish would be seen increasingly as set apart by visible conduct and appearance. This development coincided with national self-satisfaction that accompanied the working out of the United States Manifest Destiny through geographical expansion.

Manifest Destiny was another aspect of Calvinist belief. It held quite simply that the Anglo-American was predestined by God to inherit the entire American continent. Beginning with the "noble experiment" in New Jerusalem (Salem, Massachusetts), the "City on the Hill," this new breed would spread over the entire land mass of the Americas, displacing indigenous people, and buying out or running off French and Spanish land holders in their inevitable march of progress. The inheritors of Manifest Destiny, it must be remembered, were white, Anglo-Protestants and they took steps to insure that the distinctions between them and others, whether religious or racial or quasi-scientific, were constantly emphasized to prove that they were deserving of this gift. Wrote one newspaper editor:

> We are believers in the superintendence of a directing Providence, and when we contemplate the rise and amazing progress of the United States, the nature of our government, the character of our people, and the occurrence of unforeseen events, all tending to one great accomplishment, we are impressed with a conviction that the decree is made, and in the process of execution, that this continent is to be but one nation...

Even the highly respected Ralph Waldo Emerson would write that

> Men gladly hear of the power of blood or race. Everybody likes to know that his advantages cannot be attributed to air, soil, sea, or to local wealth, as mines or quarries, nor to law and tradition nor to fortune, but to a superior brain, as it makes it more personal to him.

THE SCOURGINGS, BRANDINGS AND HANGINGS

In September 1847, the Americans put the Irish soldiers captured at the Battle of Churubusco on trial. Forty-eight were sentenced to death by hanging. Those who had deserted prior to the Declaration of War were sentenced to whipping at the stake, branding, and hard labor. Most American historians contend that the punishments were neither particular brutal nor unusual given the fact that there was no prescribed code.

However, clear documentation exists that the codified Articles of War (1821) and De Hart's Practice of Courts-Martial (1847) governed courts-martial at that time and clearly stipulated the exact punishments these soldiers should have received. The Articles of War stated that the penalty for desertion and/or defecting to the enemy during time of war was death by firing squad. Hanging was reserved only for spies (without uniform) and for "atrocities against civilians." Nevertheless, forty-eight of the San Patricios were hanged: sixteen on one day in San Angel, two the following day and a larger group of thirty in a place called Mixcoac on a hill overlooking Chapultepec Castle.

Desertion prior to a declaration of war was punishable by ONE of the following punishments: branding on the hip in indelible ink, fifty lashes, or incarceration at hard labor. However, the San Patricios received more than fifty lashes, "until their backs had the appearance of raw beef, the blood oozing from every stripe," according to one American witness. In addition the punishment was administered by Mexican muleteers who were threatened with the same lash if they did not "lay it on with a will." These same Irishmen were also branded with "D" for deserter on the cheek by a red-hot branding iron, **and** they were sentenced to imprisonment at hard labor.

The sentence of the court, according to the Articles of War, should always be carried out promptly. "To prolong the punishment beyond the usual time would be highly improper, and subject the officer who authorized or caused such to be done, to charges." In the case of the last of group of thirty San Patricios to be hanged, this Article of War was cavalierly ignored.

THE HANGINGS BY COLONEL HARNEY

General Winfield Scott had chosen an officer who had been twice disciplined for insubordination as his executioner of the last group of thirty San Patricios to be hanged. Colonel William Harney had been soldiering for almost thirty years and had become notorious for his brutality. During the Indian Wars he had been charged with ravishing Indian girls at night and then hanging them the next morning after he had taken his pleasure. In St. Louis, Missouri he had been indicted by a civilian court for the brutal beating of a female slave which resulted in her death. The choice of Harney as executioner of the San Patricios seemed calculated by the American high command to inflict brutal reprisals on the Irish soldiers. Harney would not disappoint them.

At dawn on September 13, 1847, some days after the first group of twenty-eight had been executed, Harney ordered the remaining San Patricios to be brought to a hill in Mixcoac a few kilometers from Chapultepec Castle where the final battle of the war was to be fought. Observing that only twenty-nine of the thirty prisoners were present, Harney asked about the missing man. The army surgeon informed the Colonel that the absent San Patricio had lost both his legs in battle. Harney, in a rage, replied: "Bring the damned son of a bitch out! My order was to hang thirty and by God I'll do it!"

After the guards dragged Francis O'Conner out and propped him up on his bloody stumps, nooses were placed around the necks of each of the men and they were stood on wagons. Harney then pointed to Chapultepec Castle in the distance and told the prisoners that they would not be hanged until the American flag was raised over the castle signifying that the Yankees had won the battle.

The prisoners yelled out in incredulity and protest. Some made jokes and sarcastic remarks trying to goad the unstable colonel into giving an impulsive order. One prisoner asked Harney to take his pipe out of his pocket so that he might have one last smoke. Then, with a glint in his eye, he asked if the colonel would not mind lighting it with his "elegant hair."

The redheaded Harney did not appreciate the joke. He drew his sword and struck the bound prisoner in the mouth with the hilt, breaking several of the man's teeth. The prisoner was not intimidated, however. Spitting out blood and broken teeth, the irrepressible Irishman quipped: "Bad luck to ye! Ye have spoilt my smoking entirely! I shan't be able to have a pipe in my mouth as long as I live."

Meanwhile the Battle of Chapultepec raged on. Finally, at 9:30 a.m. the Americans scaled the walls of the castle, tore down the Mexican flag, and raised the Stars and Stripes. With that, Harney drew his sword and "with as much *sang froid* as a military martinet could put on," gave the order for execution. The San Patricios, after four and a half hours of standing bound and noosed in the 90 degree sun, were finally "launched into eternity."

Harney's violation of the Articles of War requiring prompt execution did not result in charges being brought against him. Rather, his behavior was rewarded. A month later Harney was promoted to Brigadier General and accompanied the Commander-in-Chief in a triumphal march in Mexico City.

The punishments ordered for the San Patricios and the way they were carried out expressed more than the judgment of the court. They smacked of contempt and repulsion indicative of religious and racist reprisals. In spite of the fact that over 5,000 U.S. soldiers deserted during the Mexican War, only the San Patricios were so punished, and only the San Patricios were hanged.

THE CONQUEST OF MEXICO AND CELTIC-AMERICANISM

Fueled by Manifest Destiny and its concomitant of racial and religious animosity, the American government dictated terms to the Mexicans in the Treaty of Guadalupe Hidalgo in 1848. Over two thirds of Mexican territory was taken, one half if one included Texas, and out of it the United States would carve California, Nevada, New Mexico, Arizona, Utah, Wyoming and parts of Kansas and Colorado. It was a profitable American adventure, a conquest to put Napoleon to shame, and all done in the name of democracy and Manifest Destiny.

Among all the major wars fought by the U.S., the Mexican War is the least discussed in the classroom, the least written about, and the least known by the general public. Yet, it added more to the national treasury and to the land mass of the United States than all other wars combined.

After the war, so much new area was opened up, so many things had been accomplished, that a mood of self-congratulation and enthusiasm had begun in the U.S. The deserters from the war were soon forgotten as they labored in the gold fields of California, homesteaded in California or, as the 1860s approached, put on the gray uniform of the Confederacy or the blue of the Union. Prejudice against the Irish lessened, as the country was provided with a "pressure valve" to release many of its new immigrants westward.

As Irish veterans returned from the Civil War and gained political power, they began increasingly to be seen as a branch of the white race (Celtic American) by the so-called scientific theorists who had previously denied them that privilege. Irish in the United States, anxious to be assimilated, gladly accepted the new designation. Ironically, the American-Irish would be among the first to disassociate themselves from the San Patricios and promote the notion that it was not an Irish battalion at all!

COMMEMORATIONS

Each year commemorations are held in San Angel in Mexico to honor the Irish who died in the War. A marble plaque in the town square reads "In Memory of the Irish Soldiers of the Heroic Battalion of San Patrick Who Gave Their Lives For The Mexican Cause During the Unjust North American Invasion of 1847" followed by the names of 71 of the men. A color guard of crack Mexican troops marches forward with the Mexican and Irish colors to a spine-jarring flourish of drums and bugles. The "Himno Nacional" is then played, followed by "The Soldiers Song." Students and dignitaries place floral tributes on the paving stones, and a honor roll is called of the fallen soldiers as the crowd collectively chants after each name, *¡Murió por la patria!* "He died for the country!" In Clifden, Galway, the birthplace of John Riley, a similar ceremony is held each September 13th.

For most Mexicans, solidarity with the Irish is part of a long tradition. There is in both countries an emphasis on the spiritual center in the family, and a non-materialistic viewpoint whereby a person's worth is determined not by what he owns but by the quality of his life. And if Paddy and Bridget, like José and María, were considered incapable of being assimilated into Anglo-Protestant society, their acceptance into Mexican society was seamless. In the words of John Riley, written in 1847 but equally true today, "A more hospitable and friendly people than the Mexican there exists not on the face of the earth… especially to an Irishman and a Catholic."

Riley sums up what cannot be clearly documented in any history: the basic, gut-level affinity the Irishman had then, and still has today, for Mexico and its people. The decisions of the men who joined the San Patricios were probably not well-planned or thought out. They were impulsive and emotional, like many of Ireland's own rebellions—including the Easter Uprising of 1916. Nevertheless, the courage of the

San Patricios, their loyalty to their new cause, and unquestioned bravery, forged an indelible seal of honor on their sacrifice.

THE HIDDEN GARDEN

Going Back To Bisbee by Richard Shelton. University of Arizona Press (Tucson, 1992). 329 pp.

Several years ago Ed Abbey, the renegade naturalist, spoke to my graduate seminar about the particularities of the Sonoran Desert. In the course of his remarks he mentioned a "hidden desert garden" right on the Arizona campus which only those who had learned to observe "with a quiet expectancy" would discover. I looked for that garden for the better part of a month. Then one day, as I was resting on the lush grass of the quad, I saw a clump of head-high brush at the far end of the field. Something the mower missed? I wondered, recalling the Frost line. Approaching it I found a narrow opening and inside a startling arrangement of green-stemmed paloverde, spindly-armed ocotillo, barrel cactus, creosote, and a small pool opposite a narrow stone bench. Unknown to the twenty thousand students who crossed the quad each morning, I often meditated there in the stillness of a Sonoran peace so obviously (like Poe's purloined letter) yet secretly present.

Richard Shelton uncovers Bisbee for the reader in much the same way. With a quiet expectancy we follow him on a compelling naturalist's tour of the surrounding Mule Mountains. Later, in Blue Boy, his 1976 Dodge van, we ride down the precipitously winding road of Tombstone Canyon to the old mining town "all piled up on top of itself as if

some child had poured toy houses down the sides of the mountains."
Our circuitous one hundred-mile journey from Tucson is as much a
journey through history as through landscape. The early Spanish set-
tlers of this region, the Chiricaua Apache, the exploiters and the ex-
ploited are well-limned here. But it is the landscape which pulls it together in a poetic naturalism. Like Annie Dillard at Tinker Creek,
Shelton's powers of observation are keen. Like her, he does not general-
ize about life but finds in the thing itself a springboard into his world
and the life of the reader.

> The canyon wren is shy and coquettish with one of the sweetest voices
> found in the Southwest. I usually see canyon wrens along streams in the
> mountains, and their voices remind me of the gurgle of water over stones,
> as if they had learned to imitate that sound but with a broader range. It's
> delicious, like the echo of a song rather than the song itself, or like the
> sound of a cello coming from a distant cave.

Shelton, a poet and a Regent's professor at the University of Arizona, acknowledges his antecedents which date from the days when,
fresh out of the army at Fort Huachuacha, he taught eighth grade in
Bisbee's brick schoolhouse. Senior teachers such as gruff Mary Bendixon
and gentle Ida Power are as important here and as interesting as General Sherman, Brigham Young or William Randolph Hearst.

Bisbee is located only six miles from the Mexican boarder and
Shelton had his share of Latino students when he was teaching there in
the 1950s. His observations of them might seem idealistic in these days
of classroom violence in the United States, but they reflect my own
teaching in Mexico in contemporary times. "Courtesy to teachers was
endemic to the Hispanic culture..whatever they did on their own time,
most of the students behaved well while they were in the classroom and
were eager to please..." (That's another page we might copy from the
seldom-read and often-denigrated text called Mexican culture.)

Woven through the local history, the peculiarities of the Sonoran

Desert, and the wry humor of the inhabitants is a fierce ache for the passing beauty of the land, a passion which has informed Shelton's five books of poetry. He rails against the language of the real estate people who call land in its natural state "undeveloped, as if it were a euphemism for a woman with small breasts," and, after the land is destroyed, "we call those who destroyed it 'developers.'" As a poet, a namer, a believer in "word magic" Shelton argues that the demeaning of the land diminishes us as a people, coarsens our perceptions, cheapens our language. An open pit mine in Bisbee becomes more than an ugly rip in the once pristine landscape; it is a scar in the human consciousness which will not heal.

Miracles happen, of course. The reclaiming of the San Pedro River Valley is one. But faith in miracles is difficult to sustain in the rapidly growing Southwest. Shelton reminds us that "the need to develop and destroy is part of our heritage."

> It got off the boat at Plymouth Rock, crossed the prairies on horseback, financed railroads with land set aside for Indian reservations, tore down mountains, and brought the light to those who were in a dark and undeveloped state. If they didn't choose to see the light, it mostly killed them, in one way or another.

Lest we feel we've come beyond that, Shelton shows how in Bisbee, which is a microcosm for America, greed continues to be an integral part of the national agenda, as upscale developers and the mining company of Phelps Dodge plan a final assault on this cultural and artistic Shangri-La.

The future of Bisbee and that of the unique beauty of the Southwest is uncertain. Growth is the platform of both political parties and, as Ed Abbey once said, "unlimited growth is the etiology of the cancer cell." It may be that Shelton's book is an epitaph, that all the warnings unheeded have brought us to a place where it is no longer possible to turn back or arrest the damage. A poet of elegance and precision, he reminds us again in elegiac prose what his early poems said so succinctly: "this is the desert/it is all we have left to destroy."

Shelton as a popular poet, gives readings of his work all across the country. Sometimes he says he is approached after a reading by member of the audience

> ...who softly speak the magic words like a litany: "desert," greasewood," "saguaro," "rain." Sometimes they have tears in their eyes as they tell me where they once lived in the desert and how they can never get it out of their minds. Each time I realize that I am in the presence of a kindred spirit and that we who love the desert speak a language whose significance others cannot entirely understand. And each time I am thankful that I, too, am not an exile, that the circumstances of life have not forced me to leave the desert.

I have lived in the desert for a good part of my own life as well. Once you come to see it, learn its moods, its seasons, know the names of its plants and animals, you find yourself transformed in a spiritual way that is never undone. For many of those who live in southern Arizona, the desert fills them, it meets the psychic need that perhaps John the Baptist went in search for two millennia ago. For others, like myself, there is another step, which is to cross that border just six miles south of Bisbee and keep going. Shelton acknowledges that he has felt the same, but stopped short of taking that step. For me, it is one of the most poignant passages in the book.

> How can one help but be attracted to a culture so attuned to the sensory that it names mountain ranges after cinnamon, like the Canelos, and garlic, like the Ajos. From where I am the distances are staggering, not romantic, deceptive. I feel the need to lose myself in those distances, in that baked land of chaotic hills and valleys, of tiny villages and sprawling collections of tin, wood and adobe shacks which make up the widely separated collective farms known as *ejidos*. I know it's too late for me... and yet... maybe someday. Maybe I will give into the dream that haunted me for thirty years. A long time ago I wrote about it, and the dream

hasn't changed. Only my ability to live it has lessened. In the poem "Mexico," I said,

> something hits me like a shovel
> and I am stunned into believing
> . . . .
> and suddenly I know
> everything I need is waiting for me
> south of here is another country
> and I have been walking through empty
> rooms and talking to furniture

LOS TIGRES DEL NORTE

It is a warm afternoon. Dove calls echo sadly across the canyons of the downtown highrises. There is a trickle of Saturday afternoon traffic. At four in the afternoon it is still the time of *la comida* and the streets are mostly deserted, the businesses closed. As we leave El Centro and head east towards Tlaquepaque, the traffic swells from a trickle, to a stream, to a river of yellow taxis in various states of repair, vintage cars of the Fifties and Sixties, and a few, like my own 1978 Mercury Monarch, clearly disreputable behemoths of steel and chrome edging their way along a wall of traffic that rises towards the outskirts of the city. We are headed for Salón Río Nilo, literally "a room on the Nile River", where the *norteno* group, Tigres del Norte will be playing to a packed house. Many people, like our landlady's cook, have saved for months to attend this concert. For many, the tickets represent a week's wages.

As the traffic swells and slows, we are able to take in the neighboring cars and passengers. There is a scattering of license plates from Texas, New Mexico, Sonora, and D.F. (Mexico City). To our right is a 1966 metallic blue Chevy Impala with Tijuana plates. It rides high in the back from oversized shocks. A push of a button and the car bucks like a bronco as ranchera music blasts from the stereo. Inside are *cholos*, tough guys, with black shirts, black Levis and fedoras. Their Spanish, which I hear through the open car window, is raucous and coarse. The delicate Jaliscan syllables are sharpened, laced with *pocho* terms. Their ladies, dressed in a similar fashion, have teased hair and used a heavy hand with their makeup. They remind of me of the *pachucas* of an earlier generation. They are girls whose startling black eyes and delicate coffee complexion has been deliberately hardened. Green eye shadow and red blush has wrested the youth from their faces. Cynicism and weariness darkens their eyes.

Passing us on the left is a '58 Ford Fairlane, black, with maroon upholstery. It has California plates and the chicano riding shotgun boasts a Virgin of Guadalupe tattoo on his right arm. The driver is wearing a black Stetson, *estilo norteño,* the peak twisted and curved down at a rakish angle. To my right the Impala rears up like a prancing stallion and the boys inside whistle to some girls they've spotted.

"¿Que onda, guapas? A donde van?"

We move on before we can hear the girls' response. As we turn at the IMSS (social security) building, the foot traffic begins to spill over the sidewalk and onto the road. There are people of all ages, although the majority seem to be young women between thirteen and twenty who walk in groups. We see few couples. Teenage boys walk in packs. Some older women who look like domestics, and many Indian girls dressed in bright red and green dresses follow them in tight-knit groups. The sound of norteña music blasts from most of the car radios. It is a rollicking, high stepping, swinging music that you could drive with to all the way to Quintana Roo, if the roads were good and you could afford the gas.

Unconsciously, I have been keeping the beat on the steering wheel. Now I look over at Lucinda and smile. We have always liked this music from the first time we heard it in the Mission District of San Francisco. We knew then that we would probably spend some time in Mexico, at least as visitors. I don't think either of us would have guessed in those days that our visit would stretch into a ten-year commitment.

This concert is by way of a peace offering and a celebration. We have had our troubles. It is difficult enough for two people working at the same job eight to ten hours a day. But when you throw in the exigencies of life in a foreign country and the death of a child, even the best of relationships become strained. Lately, the troubled days have lasted longer than usual, caused no doubt by something I said, or didn't say and, immersed in sorrow or the preoccupation with self, we drifted though some pretty bleak days. But tonight is one of music and, hopefully, a rekindling of romance and belief in the future. A tall order for a norteño concert out in the boondocks.

While teaching at Colegio Americano, we discovered that our taste in music was considered déclassé by our colleagues and friends. Norteña music as well as the ranchera music (Mexican Country) is considered the music of farmers, peasants and the lower classes. Mexican teachers gave us polite but condescending glances when we talked about it; our students were more direct.

"You've got to be kidding, Dr. Hogan," said Alejandra, an intelligent and usually tactful 11th grader when I told her that we were going to the concert.

"No, I really like their music."

"But, it's so, so… CRUDE," said Alexandra, at loss for a stronger word to express her disappointment at the taste of her English Lit teacher.

But crude is merely a word used by a rising middle class to disassociate themselves from what will one day be acceptable. I remember the same reaction to country music from my parents and their friends. An attitude we adopted in high school but were to reject in college. In Newport, R.I. where I grew up, it was called "sailor" music or "swabbie" music because the servicemen often played it in bars. My father referred to it as "cowboy" music and used to sing in a nasal twang a "heartfelt" ballad to an imaginary horse which could make us all laugh. But whether it was Hank Williams, Jimmy Rogers or Woody Guthrie, it was music associated with the bottom layer of society, the disenfranchised, the white trash, those outside the system. Like the blues, it told of what was lost, what you could expect in life, and how just plain folks could survive anyway on dreams, on hopes. Overly sentimentalized, often simplistic in lyric, nevertheless it was to capture the mainstream of the U.S. It became our folk music of the Sixties and our truest ballads of the Seventies and Eighties.

Norteña music is like that too. It also has lyrics about love lost, about grinding poverty, about getting drunk, about the police who are always the enemy of the poor. But it, too, is survival music. Because in the rollicking beat of the Mexican accordion and guitars, there is also a language of hope that is felt along the blood. The hope of solidarity in the family, the belief that no matter how bad things get there is always the release of the fiesta, the undiscovered love around the corner, the oblivion of tequila, and the gentle laying down at the end. There is also in the norteña music (as in U.S. country music) an underlying sense of value, a love of one's roots, of family, and beneath that, a genuine faith in God. A faith so sure, so unshakable, that it does not have to be articulated and seldom is.

As we get closer to what appears to be a large enclosed stadium like the Astrodome, the traffic slows to a crawl and youngsters try to direct us to parking spaces in their front yards, or to vacant lots, down side lanes. We drive past the stadium and go about a kilometer then make a U-turn and head back. The event is not scheduled until 8:00. Plenty of time for any nocturnal activity in Mexico. And this, we will discover as the night goes on, is an understatement.

There are street vendors selling the ubiquitous Chiclets, the Adams trademark which is almost a monopoly in Mexico since the days of General Santa Anna who made the first foray into chewing gum development. But there is also Wrigley's Juicy Fruit, and there are bags of peanuts, Hershey's bars, *tacos, tostadas, pan dulce*, Coke, Tigres del Norte t-shirts, stuffed tigers, black felt hats with elaborate feathered hatbands, autographed pictures of the group, and a line of people waiting to get tickets which stretches for a quarter mile down the road.

Like most lines (*colas* or *filas*) in Mexico, this one is orderly and good-humored. People do not, as a rule, cut lines in Mexico. They stand in place, wait their turn. They are not resigned or sheepish, a thought that might occur to the more impatient and aggressive North Americans who view this phenomenon for the first time. On the contrary, they are lively and self-entertaining; happy to be discussing the weather with a neighbor, drinking a *Coca*, playing with their children. They know that they will be inside sooner or later, and they know (as we have not yet guessed) that no matter how late they are getting in, the performers will arrive at least an hour after they're inside.

We find a parking space in the lot of the stadium itself. No charge for parking—at least going in. Exiting, we will, of course, be asked for a "cooperación" (a gratuity) from the attendant. There are several policemen in and around the parking lot which makes us feel secure about our vehicle. Above the lot and in front of the stadium are Jalisco State Police trucks with dozens more officers who will be deployed in the concert hall itself to protect those who wish to enjoy the music from the rowdy element who always come to events like these to see how much trouble they can get into.

On our way to the end of the line we check out the vendors' stands. I buy Lucinda one of the black Stetson hats (without the feather arrangement which costs an additional $10), and we each get a *Coca* poured into a plastic bag with a straw so that we do not have to pay a deposit on the bottle. Most of the people in line are working class families. Many in their twenties and thirties. There are a few groups of teenage girls in simple but colorful print shifts, and a scattering of young men who are quiet and dignified and dressed in clean Levis and cowboy shirts. No sign of the Tiajuana *cholos* we passed on the way, nor the chicanos from California. We would later discover that they had gone to have several rounds of drinks to "get a buzz" because of the prohibitive cost of drinks inside the concert hall.

It is about 8:15 by the time our line winds around to the front of the building and merges with three more at the front entrance. There are four turnstiles and two uniformed guards at the end of each. Female officers search the women coming in; male officers search the men for drugs, weapons, alcohol. They are polite but embarrassingly thorough.

The air is electric with excitement. There is recorded *ranchera* music playing on the loud speakers and the cement floors are scoured clean and freshly sprinkled to keep down the dust.

We are swept in with the crowd of several thousand fans down the dimly-lit corridors (which have the ambience of those of a football stadium or a bull ring) to the Salón Río Nilo. It is an enormous open cement area partly covered by sections of tin roof. The place is cavernous. It looks like a extra-large airplane hangar, one that would house a half dozen 727's. At each end, perhaps 600 yards apart, are two large stages. In addition, there are two more stages on either side of the stadium.

The furthest of the end stages has steel scaffolding erected fifty yards in front of it. Here there are t.v. cameras, monitors, sound equipment, recording devices, Televisa cameras and large speakers. There are also a large number of baffles for acoustics raised over and in front of the stage.

Along each side of the stadium are stands where one can buy roasted chickens, Mexican steak dinners, hamburgers and hot dogs, tacos, Cokes, all fairly inexpensive. A Mexican steak dinner, for example, with beans, rice and tortillas, is four dollars. But the Corona beer costs $5 for a small cup, and a mini-bottle of Barcardi rum cost $20. Each bottle contains about two shots of alcohol, and costs twice as much as the concert tickets. Few people, I think to myself, can afford to get drunk here tonight. And that, of course, is the organizer's strategy. No one in Mexico would ever think of making a rule that one cannot drink at a concert, or limiting the number of drinks. The people would not stand for it. But to make the drinks so prohibitively expensive that few could afford them, eliminates the rowdy element from the heavy partying. At least that is the plan.

By 10:30 p.m. we have circumnavigated the vast sea of people. The crowd has grown exponentially in the past two hours. While most of the periphery is covered by tin roofing material and acoustical baffles, the central portion where dancing will take place is open to the elements. Fortunately it is not yet the rainy season. It is instead a cloudless night and the stars this far from the city appear in myriads.

By 11 p.m. the stage closest to the entrance is showing signs of activity. Speakers are moved about, instruments appear, curtains and decorations are brought on stage. Multicolored spotlights flash by the technician as he tests the mikes. "*Soo—ee, soo-ee, una dos tres.*" Finally, as the crowd (swollen now to about 10,000) inch closer to the stage, the first group appears. CAÑA VERDE! Dressed in colorful charro-like outfits of purple with silver trim, they play a rollicking number which sounds much like a polka. Caña Verde is a "banda." A "banda" (as opposed to a "grupo" like Tigres Del Norte) contains a tuba, in addition to the customary bass, rhythm guitar, drums and accordion. It is the tuba which gives the "band" its distinctive "ooompa, ooompa" beat which for old time polka fans sounds a bit like Bohemian or Austrian music. But Caña Verde has trumpets as well (four of them in fact!) and when they kick in it is unlike anything we've heard before. Incredibly loud, even if the amps didn't carry at full peak for the length and breadth of six football fields, it literally makes the cement floor vibrate. The sound of the tuba and drum seems syncopated to one's heartbeat so that the heart and its valves move in one's chest with the music's sprung rhythm. It is powerful, compelling, sensual.

Here everybody dances. Two couples in their late sixties who could comfortably be guests on the Lawrence Welk Show spin across the floor in a free-style polka. Couples in their forties move to a modified version of Western Swing with broad arm movements and heel kicks. Small groups of girls do a *jarabe* dance: forming a small circle, holding hands, and them moving in and out to the beat of the music. Younger couples do a combination of Dirty Dancing and Western Swing and it is this latter that Lucinda and I settle on as we join in.

The song goes on and on. It has much more in common with aerobic exercise than ordinary dancing. Dance numbers here are not two and a half or three minutes (the duration of most U.S. records). They may last seven, eight, even ten minutes as the lead singer composes (Homer-like) impromptu verses to a *corrido,* or turns with a flourish to let the tuba (or the trumpets or the drummer) do a flourish, a solo, or a change of pace. After two of these dances Lucinda and I retire to the side lines for a cold drink and a breath of air, feeling new muscles ache from the knee bends and kicks, the dips and swings, that the music commands from even the most unrthymical body.

It is well that we have stopped though. Wiping the sweat from my forehead with an oversized *pañuelo*, I look at Lucinda. Her eyes are shining with excitement. He face is glowing with the heat, the exertion; her brown hair with gold highlights curves down over one eye. The black Stetson is sensually tilted over the other. Green-eyed lady of the lowlands here on the central plateau of Mexico dancing to the Jaliscan beat.

There is nothing cuter than a girl in a cowboy hat. And, travel where you will all over this wide world, you will find nothing sexier than a girl in tight black Levi's tucked into a pair of hand-tooled Western boots. I can feel her thigh muscles ripple as I pull her close. Ah, Tlaquepaque were paradise enow!

At midnight, following a loud but indifferent performance by a group called Liberación, the stage on the left comes alive with fire-crackers, rockets, and great streamers of sparks which would easily have set the place on fire if there were anything flammable. As it is, many of the sparks have landed in the crowd and there is some screaming as young girls try to brush each other's clothes off, and young boys gallantly assist them. Others yell, "¡*Fuego, fuego!*" and jump up and down.

As the crowd settles down, a path is made, and one of the performers, *El Colorado*, who is crippled from the waist down, is carried to the stage. He receives an ovation as he settles himself with the bass guitar and the stage darkens dramatically.

A puff of multicolored smoke and they appear in lavishly designed Western outfits. Their jackets are tailored in brocaded gold cloth. Their white pirate blouses are open at the collar, and the pants are form-fitting and fringed. Their Stetsons are worn at an arrogant angle and their hand-crafted fawn leather boots cost more than a schoolteacher makes in a month. This group, composed of three brothers, *hermanos* Ayala, and a friend, is the noisiest and most colorful I have ever seen in Mexico. They are a local favorite called Los Humildes. A friend we had met earlier during the Liberación performance, a chicano named Hector, joins us. He is from Chicago, a farm laborer turned mechanic who left Mexico ten years ago because he could not make a living. Now, his skills have netted him enough money to build a house for his mother in Jalisco and pay for vacation trips like this one every two years. He is quick-witted and has been out of Mexico long enough to appreciate some of the ironies.

"Some name, huh? Los Humildes. *Mejor se llaman 'Los Ostentosos'*"

The Ostentatious Ones! Perfect! I laugh in agreement. There is nothing humble at all about this group; nor are they the common folk their name implies. From the first number, however, I recognize their music. I have heard it often on the radio as I drive to work. The crowd goes wild. It reminds me of the old days when the Beatles first appeared. Girls screaming and jumping about. People waving their arms in the air like praising the Lord at a revival meeting.

Los Humildes is one of the fastest rising names in the Grupero Movement. The Tigres Del Norte's lead guitarist, Eduardo Hernández, has even appeared with Eleazar the accordian player for Humildes in a recent issue of the major *grupera* magazine, *Bombazos*. That's the equivalent of having Willie Nelson appear with a country singer from Canada. Plus, Los Humildes are the ones who are opening for Los Tigres – first position.

Halfway though their set we feel the surge of energy in the crowd. For many, Los Humildes are who they came to see. Los Tigres are, after all, unapologetically *del norte*. Their popularity is greatest in New Mexico, California, Arizona, Sonora. Los Humildes are considered *más mexicanos* even though, ironically, they hail from Modesto, California, while Los Tigres, four of whom are brothers, first began playing together twenty years ago in their native state of Sinaloa.

The crowd, swollen now to 20,000, has turned the dance floor into a combat zone. Even the gentlest seem to have picked up some of the elements of slam dancing. Most of the people know the songs, so they are singing along as well. *"Para no pensar en ti/Voy a ir muy lejos, lejos..."* which I recognize as one of the songs currently on the top ten. It is followed by the ardent love song *"Por Dentro Y Por Fuera,"* the title piece of their new album, then the lively *"Ojos De Yerbabuena."*

The Los Humildes set lasts for about an hour but it is so captivating, so energetic and so responsive to the audience that it seems much shorter. Following a tough rendition of *"Por Dios Que Te Mato,"* they exit the stage in an explosion of white, red and green smoke, the colors of the Mexican flag. Despite cries from the crowd of *¡Una mas! ¡Una mas!* they do not return for an encore.

"Los Tigres are going to find that hard to beat," I say to Hector.

"Ah, but the Tigres are the Tigres, amigo. They do not have to beat anyone or anything. They are already there. You'll see."

I would not have believed it was possible to have crowded more people into the stadium. But ten minutes later another five thousand fans had squeezed into the narrow gaps between those of us already there. Now we were literally up against each other's backs. The heat and humidity of that many people (pushing 30,000 now) crammed together is enough to make anyone faint and some do. The crush of the crowd towards the stage is inexorable and a bit frightening. We are pushed and shoved until we are about fifty feet from the stage. I hold on tightly to Lucinda and plant my feet. Her expression is one of grim tolerance that can, I know, slide easily into panic. I recall another time in San Francisco when an enormous crowd attended the Chinese New Year's parade. When the gargantuan firecracker dragon started exploding and the smoke and pungent odor of gunpowder filled the air, she panicked. A vacuum of oxygen-robbed air caused her to pale and lean dizzily against me. Fortunately, we were able to get out of the crowd where she could breathe. I feel that it would not be so easy with this crowd. We are surrounded by thousands of people hundred of yards deep. There are no gaps in the crowd and no escape routes.

Now the announcer is giving his introduction in a rhyming series of couplets. The amps are too close for me to make out what exactly is being said. Something to the effect that the next group is the one "we all adore," they are "the poets of the *frontera,*" and that "they love the people of Jalisco as much as we love them."

Then, *"¡Les presento a Los Tigres del Norte!"* and the lights come up on the stage. Here they are in electric blue western suits and white boots. The screams and cheers from the crowd are deafening. This is what they've come here to see and hear. Paul Eluard, the French surrealist, once said, "There is another world, and it's in this one." Now, from the visual to the aural, the main stage of Salón Río Nilo is in fact another world. There are large stuffed tigers on either side of the stage, saguaro cacti (one with a cowboy hat on its outstretched limb), western saddles on fence posts, and an enormous brown and white cow. The motif is definitely Norte—there are no suguaros down here, they are mostly in Arizona and Sonora. But this combination of the farm, the North, the cowboys, the surreal tigers, is what makes Los Tigres unique.

Voy a cantar un corrido... is how they begin. They are singing a story about a young lad from Sinaloa, Hector Félix Miranda, who is betrayed and killed. This is not one of their new *éxitos* or hits. It is an old song, a traditional *corrido* which the old timers in the crowd recognize. *Corridos* are similar to the early Anglo-Saxon ballads in intent and effect. They are narrative poems which usually have a refrain and a definite rhythm. They tells stories of heroic deeds, escapes from the law, treason, death, and lost love. Most of the Mexican *corridos* originated during the Mexican Revolution (ca. 1910-1920) and are about Pancho Villa, Francisco Madero and other heroes. But many are about lesser known figures like Arnulfo González and Valentine Félix, who faced with courage the terror tactics of the vicious *rurales* (state police) under Porfirio Díaz and the depredations of their villages by the federal troops.

In addition to a large repertoire of traditional *corridos*, the Tigres also have a number of more recent ones about *mojados* (wetbacks) who have outwitted the border guards; others about chicanos wrongly imprisoned, or locked away for years because of information provided by a *soplón* (informer).

The Tigres also sing *baladas tropicales, cumbias, rumbas, guajiras,* as well as the popular *ranchera* music which is their trademark in the *norteño* style. Their lyrics, as in "America" are thought-provoking and pointed. *Todos somos Americanos*, they sing. "We are all Americans: Mexicans, Cubans, Guatemalans, Salvadorans..." Another tune, *La Tumba del Mojado* ("The Grave of the Wetback") is a reminder that often neither the government nor the people of the north were friendly to immigrant people.

Sometime after the second tune we have managed by gentle push-ing and shoving to extricate ourselves from the crowd closest to the stage. This proved to be easier than I had originally expected because so many people obviously wanted to be in close proximity to the per-formers—a position we were willing to relinquish since the volume of the amps closest to the stage made the lyrics unintelligible. There was little aggressive pushing, though, something worth noting, despite the fact that there were gang members in the crowd, some rough looking *cholos*, and a few late arrivals who had obviously been imbibing. And, while the police presence at the concert was large and made itself felt, the crowd had a great deal of internal control. Even with the mad rush to get closer to the stage, the pushing was enthusiastic and friendly, never threatening or ugly.

Although Los Tigres have been accused by their critics in the U.S. media for glorifying smugglers and making heroes out of Mexican *traficantes*, ironically their songs also carry an anti-drug message. The difference between their message and that of traditional U.S. propa-ganda is that the Tigres' message is generally accompanied by cultural digs as well. Now they are playing *Las Drogas* where they list in rhyme (easy to do in Spanish: *aspirina, cocaina*) all the abused drugs in the United States including over-the-counter medicines, prescription diet pills, tranquilizers and mood suppressors. The drug problem, they seem to suggest, is not one created by illegal cartels and Mexican smugglers but by the demand of U.S. society for the quick fix, whether physical, emotional or spiritual.

We have been heading slowly toward the exit. It about four in the morning and it is a long drive home. In addition, we know that the traffic will be brutal if we wait until the concert ends. But now the Tigres have begun playing a beautiful old spiritual. It could be waltzed to, if there was space, but there is none. Still, it would be a shame to have been here and not danced at all to a Tigres song. We put our arms around each other and move slowly to the familiar strains of *Un Día a La Vez. One day at a time, Sweet Jesus, that's all I'm asking of you.* This number, echoing not only an old Protestant hymn but also A.A. (which numbers over a million members in Mexico) brings a message of changing what one can, but also accepting life on life's terms, in a powerful and evocative tune. It is a message we need to be reminded of on occasion. As we "dance" to it, bumping occasionally into other people who are attempting to move a step or two in the dense crowd, I look around at the sea of faces. We are the only *gringos* I have seen here tonight and yet we both feel as perfectly at home as if we were at a bluegrass concert in North Carolina or Irish festival in Connecticut. "One day at a time, Sweet Jesus…" and thank you for this one.

It is a good time to leave. The Tigres have captured the crowd and few fans will be exiting before the concert ends. The group's bond with the crowd is understandable. Los Tigres at their best are inimitable. They have one of the largest repertoires of any group in the world and they sing with heartfelt passion and joy. In addition, they are extremely talented musicians. Among their composers, Pancho Varga and Enrique Franco are outstanding contemporary folk poets. Their lyrics not only sing well but they read well.

Los Tigres are lively, authentic showmen who have an easy rapport with their audience. They stretch the mind and the heart of the listener and do more than any other group to integrate the old Mexico with the new, to preserve the roots of those uprooted by the search for economic freedom, and to prove that cultural survival, pride and integrity do not have to be sacrificed in the transition.

A policeman at the exit smiles at us and asks rhetorically if we are really leaving so early. It is almost dawn. But I do not say this. Instead I smile and say, "Yes, it is early but we have a long way to go."

Lucinda and I talk in low voices as we drive out of the parking lot.

The cool streets of Tlaquepaque are gray and still with that strange, other-worldly false light of dawn. The Mexicans call this time *la madrugada*. It is a time when objects are just beginning to discover themselves, when the eucalyptus appears as if by magic on the side of the road, and the mist hangs heavy over the fields.

As we approach the city, the buildings and towers seem to rise up out of the darkness like ships appearing in the fog. We encounter them with the sense of wonder and incredulity with which the first people of this land must have seen the Spanish masts appear in a tranquil bay. We drive past the quiet fountains and the pale rose gardens, past the bougainvillea-covered walls and the old ash trees. We touch each other shyly as the first blush of morning light touches the hills. Gently, as if this awakening will take a long, long time.

ISBN 1-55212929-2

9 781552 129296